Social Work and Social Work Education

Social Work and Social Work Education

M.S. Gore

RAWAT PUBLICATIONS
Jaipur • New Delhi • Bangalore • Guwahati • Kolkata

ISBN 978-81-316-0445-8

Reprinted, 2018

This edition published by arrangement with the author.

Published by
Prem Rawat for **Rawat Publications**
Satyam Apts, Sector 3, Jawahar Nagar, Jaipur 302 004 (India)
Phone: 0141 265 1748/7006 Fax: 0141 265 1748
E-mail: info@rawatbooks.com
Website: www.rawatbooks.com

New Delhi Office
4858/24, Ansari Road, Daryaganj, New Delhi 110 002
Phone: 011 23263290

Also at *Bangalore*, *Guwahati* and *Kolkata*

Typeset by Rawat Computers, Jaipur
Printed at Chaman Enterprises, New Delhi

To

the memory of my father

who healed me with knowledge,

skill and compassion

CONTENTS

ACKNOWLEDGEMENTS

The author is grateful to the following for permission to reprint some of the papers that had initially appeared in their publications:

1. Director, Publications Division, Government of India, New Delhi.
2. Editor, *Indian Journal of Social Work,* Tata Institute of Social Sciences, Bombay.
3. Editor, *International Social Work,* 345 East 45th Street, New York.

One of the papers published here has also appeared in B.N. Varma (ed.), *Contemporary India,* Asia Publishing House, Bombay. The author is grateful to the publishers for permission to include the same in this collection.

INTRODUCTION

This book brings together eleven papers and two notes written at different points of time during a ten-year period. These were mostly written for conferences and seminars, and cover different subjects in the broad areas of social work and social work education. The papers in the area of social work deal with the historical background of social work, the relationship between social work and social structure, and the broader question of what values and attitudes prevail among social workers. There is also a discussion of the role of voluntary action and of governmental planning as it relates to social activities. The papers in the area of social work education deal with the subjects of recruitment, the relationship between the professional and the auxiliary worker, the training of village level workers, and with some of the more urgent problems of social work education at its present stage of development.

The Perspective

These papers are not intended to be definitive statements of the problems dealt with. Between them they attempt to explore an area which has not been subjected to much analytical treatment in the Indian context. At the present stage a sufficient body of data which could make definitive statements possible is not available. What seems feasible, and in the long run more fruitful, is the application of an analytical framework to such impressionistic data as are available so that meaningful questions are raised and hypotheses suggested. The papers presented here, with the exception of one or two descriptive papers, attempt this.

The analytical framework used is the sociological one. It is possible to argue that, as compared to the psychologist's or the economist's point of view, the sociologist's point of view has a special relevance for understanding social work. But, the real reason for adopting this particular mode of analysis is that this is the one with which the author is most familiar.

The sociology of professions is by now a well-recognized speciality. In India it has not yet been identified and named. It is also true that the claims of social work to the status of a profession are still considered tenuous by many in India. Neither of these facts, however, makes an examination of the Indian social work scenario from the sociological perspective less pertinent or less promising.

Sociologists look upon social work as a system of relationships with its own characteristic roles and institutionalized behaviour patterns. Depending upon one's interest, many institutionalized patterns can be identified and analysed separately. The different techniques of social work, such as case work, group work, etc., can be looked upon as definite patterns; similarly, the very concept of professional social work can be differentiated from general, voluntary social work activity; foster home placement, day care, institutional services, etc. can again be regarded as patterns for observation and study. How small or large, how simple or complex the unit of our observation will be, must depend upon our interest, the accumulation and continuity of our knowledge, and also upon our empirical judgement of what is likely to be most productive from the scientific point of view.

In an unpublished, exploratory catalogue, outlining the many researchable problems in the sociology of professions, Professors R.K. Merton and William J. Goode have suggested the following as some of the major areas of study:

1. The profession itself—including such areas as the scope of professional activity, inter-professional relations, the growth of professionalization, etc.
2. The professional man—including the area of recruitment, professional education, professional role, etc.
3. Client-professional relationship.
4. The economic aspects of the profession.
5. The political organization of the profession, including professional associations.
6. Relationship between the profession and the social structure.

In such and other areas of observation the researcher must begin by stating what particular roles and role-relationships he or she has under observation, and then go on to answer a number of questions which are specifically sociological.

What are the consequences of a particular pattern of behaviour for other parts of the system of relationships? These consequences may be anticipated or unanticipated. They may be functional or dysfunctional. For example, the pattern of begging and giving as it prevails in India may under certain circumstances effectively meet the problem of indigence and may serve as a mechanism for providing a livelihood to a class of people who are taught and expected not to work for a living.

What are the requirements for the continuance of such a pattern? These requirements may relate to the functioning of other institutions, to the value system, and to the problem of motivating individuals to conform to defined roles. Thus, charity and beggary may function effectively in a society where the "community" still provides a meaningful focus for relationships and facilitates the working of checks on improvidence or exploitation.

What are the alternative forms of behaviour which may subserve the same functions for society?

Also, since the different parts of the social system are relatively integrated, variations in one are likely to affect the other. What kinds of strains arise in the pattern of behaviour under observation because of variations in the social context?

How do variations in this unit affect the rest of the system? How do these strains and problems manifest themselves in individuals and group? What are the new adaptive demands that are generated by change?

We can ask these questions about different aspects of social work and also about the relationship between social work itself and the larger social system. The exercise in raising and answering such questions is fruitful to the extent it gives an insight into the structure of social work and social work education. In some of the chapters that follow, these questions are asked explicitly; in others they are assumed to have been already posed; in all cases an effort has been made to answer them. Are the questions worth raising? I must be content to let the reader decide that for himself/herself.

So far I have argued that sociological analysis helps social workers to gain an insight into their own profession. But that is only one point of contact between sociology and social work. The other important point of contact is provided by the fact that social work is concerned with social as much as individual problems. In so far as at least some of the problems with which social workers are concerned manifest themselves at the level of the social aggregate, sociology performs an important function in helping the social worker to see the nature as well as size of the problems. It enables him/her to look beyond the symptoms for the more basic factors.

Even where the problem is that of an individual and not of a mass of people, it has often a social structural base and, again, sociology becomes an important tool in the understanding that a social worker seeks. Thus, the problems of an orphaned child, a widowed woman, or an aged person, take on meaning only to the extent that one understands the norms of a particular culture.

Finally, sociology as a generalizing science is concerned with identifying the local as different from the universal, the short-lived from the relatively stable, in problems and methods of work. It saves social workers from discovering "laws" where none exists and helps, by providing a comparative, cross-cultural perspective, in isolating the truly generic as different from the merely unique.

The Issues

The argument so far is likely to give the impression that the book is concerned primarily with establishing the effectiveness of the relationship between sociology and social work. This cannot possibly be true. All the papers put together here were written for social work groups, and I hope that they will be read at least as much for what they say as for the particular "bias" with which they say it.

The first two chapters cover somewhat the same area though from different points of view. Both of them look at the development of social work in India. The first one identifies some of the points of articulation between the social context and social work during three periods of time. The second one is more directly a historical-descriptive narrative of the same theme. In either case, there is need and scope for research which will substantiate or modify the broad assumptions made there—whether these assumptions relate to type of social work activity or to the hypothetical relationship between social work and social structure. For example, while it may be easy to point out the relationship between social structure and social problems at a given point of time, is it equally easy to argue that there is also a relationship between the former and the approach and methods of social work practice at various points in history?

The third and fourth chapters discuss this substantive area. The approach to child welfare activities and the overall philosophy of social work have undergone changes. It would appear that these changes are more a function of the knowledge of sociology. As new knowledge becomes available, our ways of tackling older problems change. The social worker uses one approach or another depending upon whether he or she is a trained or untrained social worker. There are two ways in which the social structure might influence social work practice. The social structure may determine the pace of growth of knowledge itself—even among specialists. More directly, it can make it difficult for the specialist to practise his/her skill in new ways. This has been the experience even of medical practitioners in non-literate and peasant societies. Can the trained social worker function better and with greater facility?

The fifth and sixth chapters bear more directly on this question. The professional social worker's role is a new one in our society. There is no continuity in the world of ideas in which social work has traditionally functioned and the ideas from which professional activity in social work springs. What adaptive demands does a professional worker experience? How far does he or she meet them? What are the mechanisms that might help reduce the strains inherent in the situation? The chapters give rise to these questions, but do not explicitly discuss them.

The seventh, the eighth and the ninth chapter further analyse problems in an analogous area, viz., the preparation of the professional social worker, the relationship between professional education and the training of auxiliary personnel, and the contribution of social work education to the training of village level workers. The chapter on social work education outlines the difficulties of developing an efficacious programme of education in a new profession where even the professional function has not been clearly defined or related to the cultural context, where the educator has often never practised his/her profession, and where field practice, as seen in agencies, and class instruction proceed from different premises. The chapter on the training of auxiliaries takes note of the need for sub-professional personnel in developing countries and discusses problem in relating their training to professional education.

The next two chapters discuss the important role and the problems of voluntary action in the field of social work. They are put together in sequence to serve as a counter-balance to the emphasis on the role of the professional, implicit in the preceding four chapters. The first of these two chapters emphasizes the need for voluntary effort and for a state policy in regard to such efforts. The second one suggests how voluntary agencies might to some extent further their objectives through a national conference of social work.

The last two chapters point out that the essential conditions for planning in the field of social welfare do not exist and that, in their absence, our planning inevitably takes recourse to the setting up of ad hoc targets. In the course of achieving these targets certain procedures have developed which are neither sound in principle nor fruitful in practice.

Every writer who puts together his/her papers for re-publication is to some extent being presumptuous. I cannot plead wholly innocent to this charge. But I am sufficiently realistic, if not modest, to know that, between them, the papers only scratch the surface. I can only hope that they would spur or provoke others to contribute to this field.

CHAPTER ONE

SOCIAL WORK AND THE SOCIAL CONTEXT

What is the scope of a sociologist's interest in studying the development of social work in a given country? The scope of this interest is broadly defined by the extent to which he is able to discover a relationship, on the one hand, between the particular social structure and the types of problems social work is called upon to handle and, on the other, between the social structure and the extent to which it determines the ways in which social work handles these problems. To the extent that one regards social work as an institutionalized pattern of behaviour, questions regarding the social function(s) that it subserves—the relation that it has to the social context, the ways in which this context might tend to limit or condition the perception and definition of social problems by social workers, the dysfunctional consequences that social work may have for the rest of the structure under certain conditions, the strains that this would give rise to, and the consequent adjustments that social work might make and require to be made—all these questions become pertinent and are of sociological interest.

Historically, social work began as an activity which aimed at bringing relief to individual—and sometimes whole groups—at the level of the basic physical needs of food, clothing and shelter. Later, other needs and problems were perceived

---

Earlier published in Baidya Nath Varma (ed.), *Contemporary India*, Asia Publishing House, Bombay, 1964.

and social work attempted to meet them for those who were not able to do so on their own. Since, theoretically, every society develops adequate institutionalized means for the allocation of social and economic roles and resources which have, at a minimum, the consequence of preventing destitution, the occurrence of destitution in any case is regarded as a partial failure of the institutions to meet the needs of that case. Destitution may take place on a small or large scale and may be chronic or emergent, Social work, understood as charity or philanthropy, is the mechanism to meet this marginal problem of destitution. This is a convenient framework for understanding the function of early social work in its relation to the larger social structure.

Medieval India

In medieval India, the caste system and the joint family provided the basic institutional framework of society. The caste system made occupations hereditary and joined groups of families belonging to the land-owning and service-giving categories in a relationship of mutuality of obligations to give and accept services. This mutuality also imposed an obligation on the land-owning families to help economically service-giving families in times of distress through offering credit and/or outright grants. The caste framework thus prevented some measure of destitution. The joint family built up another system or mutuality of obligations between brothers for the welfare of their wives and children. This flowed easily from the property relations. In a joint family all the sons were entitled to an equal share of the inherited property. After the death of the father, if the brothers continued to live together, they held the property jointly and equally. They were entitled therefore to equal returns from the ancestral property. If one of the brothers died, his male children would hold title to his share of the property. Acceptance of responsibility for the care of the widow and of the orphaned children was not difficult under these circumstances. But, the economic relations were also strengthened by social norms and the sense of obligation often went beyond the strict demands imposed by economic considerations. The aged father was not a dependent, since he was the owner of the family land. But even in the families of artisans, where there was often no inherited property to introduce economic compulsions, the aged father was not an unwelcome dependent. The joint family as an institution thus provided care for the aged, the ailing, the orphaned, the widowed, and the handicapped. There were, of course, always instances of human greed and cupidity proving stronger than the injunctions of social norms and the joint family did not always function smoothly as a 'social insurance corporation'. But, on the whole, it did have the consequence of keeping abject destitution to the minimum. Even today, the joint family conceals—from others as well as from the persons concerned—a good deal of underemployment and unemployment in the rural areas. While there is no individual destitution, there is a keeping down of the standard of living of all the units of the joint family.

Charity, in the sense of assistance given to persons to whom one is not socially related, was channelled through religious institutions. One gave to the temple or to the *math.** One also gave at times to a needy individual, but generally giving was institutionalized. As in other feudal societies, it took the form of support through religious institutions. Individuals and communities endowed temples and *maths* with landed properties. The income from these properties was used to feed the poor. Once a day—usually at mid-day—the temples would serve meals to whoever came and asked for them. This system of providing for the needy was known as *sadavrata.* All temples in important religious centres offered this service. At times individuals gave such meals in commemoration of their forefathers.

Yet, the really destitute person in the village community was not well provided for. He was a person without land, without the skills of an artisan, and without the hereditary rights of giving service to particular landlords. He could

*The headquarters of a religious sect.

establish no socially sanctioned relationship with anyone. One of the few ways open to him was to become a mendicant. This he did by first leaving his village and going to one of the centres of religious importance. There he joined one of the sects and sought his spiritual as well as temporal salvation. If giving was institutionalized, so was begging. Mendicancy was an avocation. For the indigent individual it was also a channel for establishing sanctioned social relations and for achieving freedom from work—quite apart from the help it gave in finding his daily maintenance.

In the urban areas—the local seats of political power—there was a certain amount of charity outside the strictly religious sphere. In ancient India during the Buddhist period, and even later, during the period of the Guptas, there were services for the aged, handicapped, and generally destitute sections of the population. Commenting on the responsibilities of the king, Kane refers to numerous sources to buttress his observation: "The king is also called upon to support helpless and aged people, the blind, the cripple, lunatics, widows, orphans, those suffering from diseases and calamities, and pregnant women, by giving them medicines, lodging, food, and clothing according to their requirements."* But it was mainly during the emergencies of famines and floods that "giving" on a large scale took place outside the religious channels. The rich and the ruling were enjoined to support the indigent. The king opened his granaries, and philanthropic individuals distributed food and clothing.

In some parts of the country there was also the custom by which poor Brahmin boys supported themselves during their student days by taking their meals once a week by turn in one of the households with which they had made prior arrangements. This system was known as *madhukari*. It was, however, usually restricted to Brahmin boys. Brahmin girls and persons of other caste groups did not have the same facility. Moreover, it was not intended to meet the problem of indigency so much as to encourage the poor Brahmin boy to continue his study of the scriptures. Thus, in medieval Indian society,

*P.V. Kane, *History of the Dharmashastras*, Vol. II.

1. The problem of indigency was mitigated largely by the particular norms of mutuality of obligations associated with the functioning of the joint family and the caste.
2. The persons whose needs could not be met within the framework of the caste and joint family relationships were the ones who had to be deliberately provided for. This provision was made through religious channels and occasionally through the secular machinery of the state.

This situation is not essentially different from that which is characteristic of other peasant societies. The role played by the obligations of the extended family in other peasant societies was similar—though never exactly the same—to the role of the joint family in India. One can also find a point of comparison between the relationship of the feudal lord and his vassal on the one hand and the *jajmani* system which defined the economic relationships between families of different caste groups on the other. It must be admitted, of course, that the obligations of the extended family in other peasant societies were never reinforced by religious and property considerations and were not nearly as institutionalized as in India.

With regard to the role of religious institutions in relieving distress and poverty, one finds that the churches and the monasteries of medieval Europe played a role fundamentally similar to that played by the temples and *maths*. Prior to the period of the Poor Laws in England, the churches and the monasteries were the chief agencies of relief. They built up properties and endowments much the same way as the temples and *maths* in India. In course of time, however, corruption and malpractices developed among the priesthood and the monks and the religious institutions did not adequately meet the problem of poverty in the countryside. In England, this along with other factors, gave rise to the organization of relief through the Poor Laws. They represent the first major effort of the secular institution of the state in tackling the problem of vagrancy and poverty. In India, one does not come across a parallel development. The sixteenth and the seventeenth centuries in India saw the outbreak of frequent and severe famines which swept across the countryside and resulted in widespread starvation and death. The kings responded with royal charity and doles, but there were no systematic efforts to meet the problem on a broad basis. There was certainly no effort to impose any rates on the citizenry in order to tackle the problems of destitution and beggary. Throughout the sixteenth, the seventeenth, and the eighteenth centuries, the only ways of handling the problems continued to be the traditional ones of individual philanthropy and religious charity. The state took no initiative in working out measures for the prevention and mitigation of destitution. Nor does one find the emergence of institutional facilities for meeting the problems of orphans, widows, the aged, etc. There were no agencies which were concerned exclusively with the administration of relief. The concept of social service as different from religious charity had not emerged. The social conscience of the individual citizen and the concern of the community as a whole for the deprived and needy sections of the population expressed itself primarily through religious channels.

The Nineteenth Century

This was the picture at the end of the eighteenth century and the beginning of the nineteenth century. But at this time some new forces were to come into play which in course of time showed up the inadequacies of the caste/joint family structure on which Indian society was based. These forces were political, economic, ideational and religious. Politically, it was the period of the consolidation of British rule and the institution of a system of administration which was characterized by central direction. The influence of the rule of the British, unlike the rule of all previous dynasties, was to spread out to remote areas through a uniform system of administration and judiciary. While this was to be instrumental in forging a new unity in the country, it had the immediate consequence of weakening the authority of the local village councils. The decisions of the village councils were no longer final and could be appealed against. The social control that these councils were able to exert was inevitably undermined. This happened at a time when economically the picture was ominous. The repeated famines at the end of the eighteenth century had upset normal economy in parts of the country. In the urban areas the artisans and craftsmen suddenly lost the support of their royal and noble patrons. The new ruling class did not have the same appreciation for the fineries of these craftsmen. Later, the economy was to be thoroughly ruined by its being made ancillary to British industry. Destitution and indigence increased manifold. The village councils were unable to impose traditional obligations. A sense of political defeat and economic insecurity sapped the sense of community. The spirit of co-operation gradually gave place to rivalry and mutual distrust. With every succeeding decade the number of litigations increased and the only profession that prospered was that of the lawyer. These changes did not occur all of a sudden. They were in the nature of a gradual process that continued through the whole century and later.

At the same time, one unanticipated consequence of British rule was that it brought people into contact with British political and social thought. The ideas of a growing democracy, ideas which preached a basic equality of human beings, ideas flowing from the upsetting of feudal estates and the rise of the urban entrepreneur—all these reached the more sensitive Indian minds and led to serious questioning and rethinking of traditional values. The activities and writings of some of the Christian missionaries added a sense of urgency to this process. The reactions were both defensive and assimilative. Both religious reform and revival followed.

From the viewpoint of social work or social service these movements were influential at two levels. One of these related to the value premise on which the traditional caste-cum-joint family structure was based. The caste structure provided for a certain mutuality of obligations between caste groups. And yet it was based upon the principles of hereditary and unequal status and unequal access to opportunities in life. This clashed with the basic tenets of liberal thought which in its original home had been fashioned essentially to break through the feudal social order and to serve as a philosophy for the 'new society' characterized by mobility of economic status and by political equality. The concept of equality of men was not entirely new or foreign to India. The *Vaishnava* saints of every generation had preached similar thoughts with varying degrees of directness. But the configuration of social and political power had never been favourable for arguing against the caste system itself. Even the British government did not directly legislate against caste; at the same time it took care not to allow itself to be limited by an acceptance of caste norms in its many policies. In fact, its policy of recruitment to administrative and military posts was so shaped that in its anxiety to keep a balance of forces it inevitably weakened the power of traditionally established castes. Nor, again, did the justice administered by British courts take cognizance of the caste status of individuals. Against this background, the social reformers of the nineteenth century attacked, first hesitatingly and then with self-assurance, the very basis of caste. They argued for freedom in the choice of occupations which were otherwise hereditarily determined and they also attacked the inequality of castes. The castes did not disappear, but the battle had been joined. The privations of the lower caste groups and the inequality of the caste system as a whole was forced upon the consciousness of all educated persons as an important social problem. It was, however, too early—for this problem to receive the attention that it deserved and had to wait for almost three quarters of a century before it was given a priority.

The other institution to be attacked was the joint family. It was criticized on the ground that it tended to make individuals dependent and robbed them of all initiative. Its smooth functioning required obedience and acceptance of the authority of elders. Its worst victim had been woman. In a household predominated by her husband's relations she was the one who had to make all the adjustments and compromises. She had no education and no claim to any property whether from her parents or parents-in-law. As a widow she became a helpless dependent. She could not remarry nor have any degree of independence in the house of her brothers-in-law.

Woman became the great object of deliverance for the social reformer of the nineteenth century. Abolition of *sati*, promotion of widow remarriage, education and rehabilitation of the young widow—these and others were the measures that had to be argued and fought for. In this area she achieved a much greater measure of success than in the area of abolition of caste distinctions.

In so far as social reform activity reflects the concern of the progressive sections of the community for the sufferings and the welfare of underprivileged groups it is of interest to the social worker and overlaps with his field of activity. As will be seen later, backward classes (i.e., groups generally lower in the caste order) and women become the two important recipients of social welfare services in the twentieth century.

Quite apart from social reform, the nineteenth century is also noted for one more development of significance for the growth of social work. The various movements of reform and revival were all usually accompanied by a social service counterpart. This was a result partly of the inner compulsions of the movement itself and partly of the need to meet the challenge of the Christian missions. As was pointed out above, the latter part of the eighteenth century, and to a degree even the earlier part of the nineteenth century, had seen the recurrence of famines resulting in widespread destitution. The Christian missions began by helping to meet the needs of the situation through relief camps, orphanages, destitute homes, etc. The Indian reform movement itself soon developed these activities.

To begin with (in the 1830s and 40s) the reformers established schools for boys and for girls. It must be realized that in the nineteenth century even the starting of educational institutions which charged little or no fees was an act of service. It was a basic need. The government of the country took no firm lead in the matter.

The establishment of schools was an act of faith and an expression of social awareness and of sensitivity to social needs on the part of a small band of forward-looking individuals. Their only gain was the satisfaction they derived from their work. The establishment of a school for girls had the further significance of being in conformity with the major preoccupation of the nineteenth-century reformers—the removal of the social disabilities of women.

But it was not only schools that they founded. They founded orphanages, widows' homes, homes for the aged and the destitute. Toward the latter part of the nineteenth century there were also a few institutions for the blind and the deaf. The development of institutional services for the needy groups was a new trend in the field. These service were to set a pattern for meeting social needs outside the institutional framework of the joint family. They were established mainly by religious but also by non-religious groups. They were gradually accepted as objects fit for channelling individual charity and philanthropy. Persons who would otherwise have endowed temples and *maths*, now began to donate funds to such institutions.

The development of institutional care is important, because it indicates a moving away from the goal of immediate and temporary relief to the goal of sustained care. It marks the development of an agency that regards the organization of care as its special and exclusive responsibility—unlike as in the case of outdoor relief organized by temples and *maths*. It has also the consequence of giving rise to a small group of persons who devote their entire time to the administration and management of these institutions of care. Some of them earn their living through this work, but a good many do it for the love of their labour.

Another development that marked the latter part of the nineteenth century was the establishment of charitable trusts and funds. Most of these trusts gave scholarships to needy students. But some of them—the larger ones—also gave doles to poor families. The organization of cash relief given to known individuals—not impersonally to any one who asked—was a totally new development. Despite all that the reformers did to point out the evils of the caste system, however, these trusts and funds were organized along caste lines. When they were not restricted to a particular caste, they were restricted to particular religious communities.

It may be noted here that the establishment of residential care institutions as well as of the funds and trusts was primarily an urban phenomenon. People came to the urban areas because their lives were influenced, more effectively than ever before, by the administrative and judicial authority located in the tehsil and district headquarters. The newly growing educated middle class, consisting of government servants, school teachers and professionals, lived in towns. The indigent and the needy migrated to the towns and cities for relief. Later, the unemployed agricultural labourer and the displaced artisan were to come to these urban centres to seek employment in the newly established commercial and industrial undertakings. It was in the cities and towns therefore that the new instruments of relief and care found their natural home. It was also in the urban areas that the inadequacy of the joint family as a system of insurance came to be increasingly experienced. It must be noted that such urbanization as had taken place was not an index of industrial growth; it was a consequence of the establishment of new centres of administration. This urbanization was characterized not by the growth of large cities, but by a multiplicity of small district and tehsil towns. It was an urbanization where the middle-level government servant set the tone of life rather than the shopkeeper or the industrialist. Such urbanization was not likely to give rise to the typically urban problems of today. But it did give rise to strains. The joint family did not break up. But it was subjected to new strains in the middle classes. The earning of an individual income which was related to one's labour and equipment rather than to one's share in the inherited property, the differentiation in the occupations followed by different brothers, the impact of English education, the higher age of marriage—all contributed to weaken the assurance with which its institutional arrangements were taken for granted. Middle-class widows sought opportunities for education in a bid to become economically self-dependent. If they could not have these opportunities while remaining in the family, they went and got admitted to institutions organized for the purpose. There was also an increase in the number of persons at the lower-income levels who got their orphaned nephews and cousins admitted to institutions rather than having them kept at home on sufferance. There was no longer the compelling bond of commonly-held inherited property to make it necessary for them to accept the responsibility for their care. The sanctions of community opinion were less rigorously operative. But even more consequential than the relative disintegration of the joint family was the disintegration of the rural economy itself which rendered an increasing proportion of the population destitute with every successive decade. This kept the institutions filled with inmates and there was always a large number still—left uncatered for.

The nineteenth century is thus noted for three developments. The first of these is the feverish activity of its untiring social reformers who broadened the social awareness of the community to recognize the special needs of women and of lower caste groups. They succeeded admirably in the former, but were far from effective in the latter. The second is the growth of residential institutions as instruments of organized and sustained care. The third is the establishing of trusts and charities as formal modes of providing outdoor relief for the needy in a more systematized fashion than ever before. Incidentally, another fact to be noted is the emergence of a group of people who devote themselves to the administration and management of these newly developed and formal instruments of care and relief. While these new forms of service developed, the earlier forms consisting primarily of religious and individual charity also continued to play their role. They continue even today, but they are no longer the only or even the main channel for the expression of community concern and social responsibility.

The Twentieth Century

The twentieth century presents a much more complex picture. By the end of the first decade, the economic and political situation had grown worse. The solutions offered by the social reformers and social service institutions appeared far too inadequate, if not irrelevant. With the appearance of Mahatma

Gandhi on the political scene the language of debate had become stronger. While social reformers and social workers were individually respected for their dedicated lives, their efforts were seen to offer palliatives rather than fundamental solutions. The fundamental solution—or at least the necessary condition for its operation—lay in political independence. Thus, the social reformers and workers were outside the main current of activity. The number of institutions grew; they also catered to newer categories of persons, but they could never expect to alter the basic situation that gave rise to want and need. The heightened sensitivity of the socially responsible individual found the channels offered by social service activity to be limiting, if not unrelated to reality.

It is in this context that one has to look at the *constructive programme* of Mahatma Gandhi. He felt that the situation of need and want was too generalized to be met by the efforts of a few devoted workers or the philanthropy of a few well-to-do individuals. What was called for was not *help* but *self-help*—self-help on the level of the entire community. The constructive programme provided the *modus operandi* for this manoeuvre of self-help on a comprehensive, community basis. The indigence and destitution of individuals was not a consequence of their particular handicap, but resulted from a basic malady characterizing the entire economic and political structure. Social work, or social service in the traditional sense, was of no avail. The situation called for a redefinition and readjustment of social, economic and political relationships.

The redefinition that Gandhi provided was based on the concept of a self-sufficient village economy where the large-scale processes of mechanization found no place. One produced for local consumption, not for an export market. The local community would reassert itself through the revival of panchayats, i.e., councils of elders, and by boycotting the agencies of central control. This seemed to many like going back to ancient civilization. Even during the lifetime of Gandhi, the acceptance of this goal by the people was not whole-hearted. Since his death the subject has lost all but academic interest. Despite this, Gandhi has left the impress of his vision. His vision of village communities working for their own regeneration on a multifaceted front has been retained and made into a philosophy—the philosophy of the Community Development Movement initiated by the government.

The relation of social work to community development is at present peripheral. This is largely because of the tendency to focus exclusively on economic targets and a failure to realize that there can be no self-help except in a community where the members have been educated to see their problems in perspective and have been motivated to action. The job of motivating the villager has turned out to be more complex than was originally conceded. The administrator must have greater orientation to the methods of working with communities and groups and here social work may have a contribution to make. Apart from the Community Development Movement, one can see the continuity of the Gandhian approach to social problems in the work of the members of the Sarva Sewa Sangh. Some of them have devoted themselves to *Bhoodan* (the land gift) movement; some others to work in the rural and tribal areas.

While it is true that Gandhi was concerned with the problems of the community as a whole, it does not mean that he did not see some groups as being specially disadvantaged even within this generally deprived community. He did accept the special claims of two groups to social conscience. These groups were women and the untouchables. He devoted the best part of his non-political activity to removing their disabilities. The disabilities of these two groups were to be traced not to the limitations of individuals but to the structural limitations of Indian society. Their disabilities were therefore in the nature of a social malady. In this way Gandhi was continuing the work of the social reformers of the nineteenth century. Under his leadership the women's movement and the movement for the removal of untouchability grew to full stature. Both the movements have gained their objectives in the political and legislative sphere. The *social* reality has not yet changed radically and there is still a great part of the way to be covered.

A third group which received special attention from Gandhi consisted of the tribal populations of India. These peoples belonging to many ethnic groups lived at different levels of economic development. Most of them lived in remote forest and hill areas. Some lived a nomadic life and a few in settled rural communities in close proximity to the rest of the population. But they were universally poor, illiterate (or, rather, pre-literate) and, in some areas, subject to the ravages of disease. Their first contacts with the agents of civilization—the forest contractors and forest officers—were unfortunate. They were economically exploited. Their problems became further complicated by the introduction of political and religious considerations. Gandhi saw the problems of the tribals as the problems of the Indian social order. As in the case of the untouchables and women, the privations of the tribals were not only a problem of material improvement but also a problem of social conscience. Under Gandhi's persuasion some bands of constructive workers went into these communities to organize services for them. Since independence, this programme has been given high priority by the government.

While Gandhi's constructive programmes and the various movements for and by socially underprivileged groups took centre stage, the quiet efforts of individual social workers continued. The categories of persons for whom services were organized increased in number. To the orphans, the widows and the aged were added the physically handicapped, the physically exploited, the beggars, the unmarried mothers, the delinquent and wayward juveniles, and, later, the mentally handicapped. The number of institutions also increased though most of them continued to be in urban areas. In addition to all these groups, in the post-independence period, the most important single problem that had to be tackled was that of the rehabilitation of refugees. This was a problem for the entire community and social workers made their own contribution towards its solution.

The developments in the first half of the twentieth century are, however, notable not only for the expansion of social work but also for some new trends that are to be noticed.

One of these has been the acceptance of the need for training and preparation for social work. The knowledge of the social sciences has brought home the complexity of the problems faced, the need for developing a scientific orientation, and some practical skills in the handling of these problems. With this the field of social work education and professional social work has grown.

The emergence of a professional group has of course raised all the usual problems of the relationship between the professional and the non-professional. The situation in social work is further complicated by the fact that the non-professional is not only "non-socialized" in professional values and skills, but is usually a person who, since he does not derive his livelihood from this avocation, considers himself to be the professional's superior in status. These problems have yet to be solved. Additionally, there are problems arising out of the fact that the model for social work education—as the models for other programmes of professional education—is largely borrowed from other countries. This gives rise to many difficulties—some of which are genuine and some due largely to prejudice. At any rate, it tends to accentuate the difference between the orientations of those who are trained and those who are untrained.

The need for adequately qualified persons who will look upon their work as a full-time responsibility can hardly be questioned. With the growth of welfare services sponsored and financed by the state it would be difficult to do without the professionally qualified and professionally oriented social workers. As it is, the contribution made by the professional workers in the planning and development of welfare services has been quite considerable at the Centre and in the states. The professionally qualified person is still generally young and occupies junior positions in planning and administrative units but he is able to make his contribution at the stage of drafting and whetting new proposals.

The contribution of the professional social worker in the non-governmental sector is so far limited. The salaries available in non-governmental agencies do not attract the best persons in the field and, besides, in this period of transition it is difficult for the professional to function with any decisiveness without seeming to take over the functions of the volunteer executive. A redefinition of the respective roles of the Honorary General Secretary and the Executive Secretary will be necessary if the two are to make their distinctive contributions.

The general acceptance—even if at the verbal level—of the need for a scientific orientation has had one consequence. It has tended to emphasize that relief—temporary and unorganized—cannot be the objective of social work activity. It has drawn attention to the need for preventive measures and to the possibility of rehabilitation. This has led to the organization of some services within the normal community. The establishment of Welfare Extension Projects and the proposal for Urban Community Development Projects are pointers in this direction. There is also an increasing emphasis on the needs of the normal child. At the same time, there are efforts to develop rehabilitative (after-care) services for those discharged from institutions.

Still another trend has been the acceptance in principle by the state of its responsibility to provide the conditions for the well-being of the citizens. Social workers in India have not had to do half the pleading and lobbying that social workers in Great Britain and the USA had to do to have this principle accepted. This is an instance of the way in which behaviour at least at the verbal level may be conditioned by the behaviour of reference groups. As will be easily noticed such transference of goals between two social groups which function at entirely different levels of technological efficiency can give rise to serious strains in the absence of comparable resources. Social work as it evolved in Western society in the nineteenth century was essentially concerned with the individual. It tended to look upon his problems as a reflection of his individual inadequacies and not of the inadequacies of the social system—at least not initially. The values on which the social system rested were implicitly accepted. They were the values of free economic enterprise, of a political system based upon democracy, and of an attitude of laissez-faire. During the whole of the nineteenth century social work was content to look upon destitution as a situation that could be adequately met by individual and later by organized philanthropy. Social workers did not associate themselves with those who tried to lay the blame for poverty, destitution, and all the other social problems at the door of the economic system and particularly its system of distribution. Even the efforts to make the state and local bodies accept responsibility for public health measures were met with rebuff as leading to interference with the life of the individual citizen. It was only in the twentieth century—and then as a consequence of two world wars—that the state accepted responsibility for protecting the individual citizen against destitution. It was also then that social work accepted the responsibility for social action. By the time the states in the Western world accepted the responsibility for social security, they had also developed the necessary resources for it.

In India, the situation is different. It would be futile to attempt to define the problem of *need* in India as the problem of the individual. On the other hand, the state does not have the resources to accept the implications of defining it in the only other way. It is not the philosophy of distribution that is holding up social security measures in India; it is the reality of low production in all the sectors of national economy. This had led to a repeated emphasis on the high priority to be accorded to economic programmes and to the avid acceptance of the important role that voluntary agencies should play in social welfare. Unfortunately, the voluntary agencies which formerly depended upon the charity of wealthy individuals who have since been chafing at the policy of progressive taxation adopted by government, have themselves begun to look more and more to the state for financial support. It is therefore not unusual to hear voluntary agencies blaming the government for its tardiness and government administrators blaming voluntary agencies for their dependence on public funds. The situation would be amusing, were it not somewhat tragic. The government administrator, situated as he is, considers voluntary agencies as an unnecessary instrumentality of action except where the agency justifies itself on financial grounds by saving the government some necessary outlay. Voluntary agencies evaluate their contribution from a different standpoint and find justification in the popular support they build up and the citizen participation they achieve. The fact, however, is that voluntariness loses much of its vigour and vitality when it is sustained largely on state support. The administrator finds it easier to create the impression of voluntariness by constituting ad hoc bodies of "non-officials". These non-officials owe their positions to the administrator and only secondarily to their organizations. The consequence is an inevitable weakening of the organizations in the field of social work. The creation of ad hoc nominated committees is dysfunctional to the development of representative organizations. The problem of the relationship between the state and the voluntary agencies is difficult even where the latter have firmly established themselves and enjoy a measure of financial independence. Where the voluntary agencies tend to become dependent upon state financial assistance, the problem of this relationship is further complicated.

A recent development in the sphere of social work is the great emphasis laid on planning. All governmental activity in the economic sphere is regulated by the rhythm of the Five-Year Plans. This has had its impact on social work. The fact that voluntary agencies have become increasingly dependent upon state resources has made it seem natural that their activities should also be synchronized with the Five-Year Plans. But planning in the field of social work is beset with difficulties. Planning to be successful requires, at a minimum, a control over the instrumentalities of action. This is difficult when in many cases the instrumentality consists of voluntary agencies which have a will of their own and whose sense of priorities is likely to be different. This again highlights the need for developing a satisfactory relationship between government administration and voluntary agencies.

The major note in the current period of the growth of social work services—in fact in the growth of all services—is struck by a realization of the limited resources available for meeting recognized needs. This is perhaps true of all countries at all times. But the needs have probably never been greater and the resources never more limited as in the economically underdeveloped countries of the world today. The international political situation adds urgency to all efforts. There is a sense of racing against time and in the heat of the struggle there is questioning of the ends and the means of action as well.

CHAPTER TWO

HISTORICAL BACKGROUND OF SOCIAL WORK IN INDIA

Social work has had a long history in India. In the title to this chapter, however, the words "historical background" are used deliberately and are intended to distinguish it from a history of social work in India. What is attempted is the presentation of the thought of some of the more important thinkers and social reformers of the nineteenth and the twentieth century with a view to showing the relation between these trends of thought and the development of social work. There is therefore no effort to recount in detail the actual occurrence of events in the field of social work and social reform.

It is necessary to begin by pointing to the obvious inadequacies that are likely to remain as a result of the absence of the ready availability of historical data. I have been guided in the presentation of the first part of this chapter by the general analysis of the development of social thought in modern India presented by the late Acharya S.D. Jawadekar in his masterly treatise, *Adhunik Bharat* (Modern India). His analysis centres round a discussion of the interaction between the religious and traditional ways of thinking of the eighteenth and nineteenth centuries and the liberal and rationalistic mode of thinking which came to the fore in the nineteenth and twentieth centuries. He tries to show the

---

Revised version of a paper first published in *Social Welfare in India*, Planning Commission, Government of India, 1955.

consequences of this interaction in the spiritual and political aspects of life. I have made an effort to spell out its implications in the field of social reform and social work.

"Social Reform" and "Social Work"

Before proceeding to a discussion of the actual content of this chapter, however, it is necessary to clarify the use of two terms—*social reform* and *social work*. Social reform aims essentially at change—a change sometimes involving the basic values of a society—whereas social work primarily relates to welfare activities undertaken within the limits set by the existing values. Social reform is naturally the field for the volunteer leader, whereas social work increasingly becomes the domain of the professional. The demarcation between these two fields is never easy. It is specially difficult in periods of transition in which new ideas and the spirit of questioning pervade the whole society. At such times, all activity—social, economic, or in the field of welfare—draws inspiration from and is influenced by the activity of the reformer.

Much of what is today recognized as the field of social work and public welfare has crystallized out of the vigorous activity of the nineteenth century reformers who perceived the inadequacies of older laissez-faire values in the context of a changing economic and technological environment. In India, the distinction between social reform and social work is particularly blurred. All work in relation to the traditionally underprivileged members of a society involves a change in the values of that society. Work with the Harijans, the scheduled castes and tribes and even welfare activities relating to women in general fall simultaneously in the realms of both social reform and social work. Fighting for the equality of rights for women, making a plea for a better deal for the Harijans, launching a movement to bring about a change in the manner of handling young offenders, are all instances of social reform activity. To run an institution for rescued women, to organize community services for the benefit of the Harijans, and to provide shelter and educational facilities for neglected and delinquent children, are instances of social work activity.

It will be seen that such distinctions are difficult in any example of concrete social work activity. Yet, conceptually, the distinction has significance because, as will be pointed out, the two types of activities call for different types of leadership and personnel. The difference also accounts for a good deal of the lack of mutual appreciation of the roles played by the voluntary and the professional personnel. We will, however, not elaborate this point here as other aspects of this question will come up for discussion at later stages in this chapter. We may only note the broad characteristics of the two types of activities. It is possible to say that social reform aims at a change of the pattern of life of a whole community while social work aims at meeting the needs of individuals and groups within the life-pattern of that community. Social reform is addressed to the change of social institutions and social work to relieving the suffering resulting from the failure of individuals and groups to function effectively within an institutional set-up. Social reform requires pioneers and leaders of public opinion whereas social work increasingly tends to depend upon trained personnel. (This last sentence may give rise to a misunderstanding that this author conceives leaders of public opinion and trained personnel as mutually exclusive categories. This is not so. The distinction, as indicated above, is conceptual rather than a distinction between persons.)

Social Service Tradition in India

With this introduction, it should now be possible to move on to a discussion of early social work activity. Our discussion is limited to the nineteenth and twentieth centuries. It may, however, not be out of place to say that service of the needy is a part of the long tradition in India. As in other familistic societies the relationships between individuals and groups were so established that the care of the needy was built into the social institutional structure. Religion also emphasized the values of charity, philanthropy and mutual help. The giving of alms and the feeding and care of the destitutes were acts of religious merit. The kings and chiefs were enjoined to provide free kitchens during famines. The temples gave shelter to the homeless. The source of this welfare activity was mainly religious. From the age of the Buddha to the twentieth century, India has had a succession of men whose source of inspiration for their humanitarian activity and preaching lay in their search for spiritual salvation. This, however, is not a unique feature of India, as is often likely to be believed. All over the world, different peoples have found inspiration for humanitarian activity in their religious teachings.

Besides this religious emphasis leading to individual actions of charity, the social institutions provided for mechanisms which would help to meet the needs of the old, the sick, and the otherwise helpless sections of the community. The joint family provided for the care of older generations as also for those of its members who were unable to make their fullest contributions to social life on account of disability. The physically handicapped, the chronically ailing, and the mentally deficient were all looked after by the family corporation. Besides the joint family, the caste and community councils often took responsibility for individuals who needed succour. The economic system was itself governed by social customs, such as the jajmani system, which made it obligatory for the high caste employers to look after the needs of the low caste employees. These social mechanisms with their customary sanctions were effective in a small rural community with its intimate, face-to-face contacts.

Influence of Christian Missionaries

It is against this background that we have to consider the impact of new ideas and laws that were enacted with the coming of the British rule. The consolidation of British rule could be said to have taken place at the beginning of the nineteenth century. (The Maratha power, the last to resist British supremacy, was completely vanquished in 1818.) Yet, the influence of a new way of thinking brought in by British and other Western missionaries, educationists and administrators was felt as early as the late eighteenth century. In Bengal, the Serampore missionaries began their activities in 1780. They were interested in evangelical work, but they were also motivated by a strong conviction that many social and religious reforms were necessary within the Hindu social structure itself. They attacked child marriage, polygamy and female infanticide, and worked for the abolition of *sati*. They argued in favour of widow remarriage and agitated against practices of human torture in worship. Besides drawing pointed attention to some of these customs, which were prevalent at that time, the Serampore missionaries made a fundamental attack on the caste system. On the positive side they tried to show how Christianity believed in the innate equality of all human beings and how it was free from the many superstitions and the rigid ritualisms that characterized popular Hinduism.

If the impact of Christian missionaries was primarily on the religious and social institutions, the English education was responsible for the introduction of a new pattern of thinking whose major characteristics were rationalism, democracy and liberalism. The activities and the preachings of the missionaries set up a defensive reaction among the Hindus. On the other hand, the rationalistic traditions of thinking, which had gained great prestige because of the developments in modern science, had an innate appeal for the Indian intellectuals. In the social as well as the religious reform movement that followed, we notice the effects of both these impacts. The conventions and forms of the joint family and the inequities of the caste system could not be reconciled with the individualistic and equalitarian trends of liberal thought imbibed by newly educated middle classes.

Changes in Economic Life

But the impact of British rule was felt not only through new ideas, but also through the imperceptible, yet equally significant, changes that came about in the economic life of the country. The economy of rural self-sufficiency was disturbed.

Our villages increasingly exported raw materials and imported finished goods. This was an economy of the growing impoverishment of rural areas. Individual villagers left the village communities with their customary obligations and travelled to the metropolis with its contractual relations. In the wake of this change came the many problems of an industrialized urban community—destitution, drinking, exploited childhood and womanhood, and slums. But urban living and Western education were also responsible for strengthening some of the democratic and liberal traditions that took root in Indian soil in the nineteenth century. They made us sensitive to needs which had not been perceived earlier, for example, the need for education, the right of women to freedom and equality in all walks of life.

There are thus three directions in which the reform and social work activities of the eighteenth and nineteenth centuries expressed themselves: the first related to the area of religious and spiritual tenets; the second to the area of customary practices, social and ritualistic; and the third to the area of new problems and needs that demanded solution as a result of urbanization. The same individual or organization would very often engage in all the three types of activities; yet the activities of the religious reformer, the social reformer and the social worker are not inseparably connected.

The same social reform goals were often pleaded for by organizations of divergent religious beliefs (for example, the Brahmo Samaj and the Ramakrishna Mission, with their basically different religious philosophies, asked for the abolition of caste); and the same social work activities were undertaken by people with divergent religious as well as social values (for example, the Christian missionaries, the Hindu religious reformists as well as the secular intellectuals—all pleaded for the organization of institutional care for the needy and for relief measures in periods of emergency). It is therefore necessary to take into consideration not only the specific activities but also the aims and objects motivating personalities and organizations in their work.

Rammohun Roy's Contribution

The first person whose life and activities should be of interest to us in a survey of social reform and social work activity is Raja Rammohun Roy. As a writer, as an educationist, as a religious reformer and as a social worker, he symbolizes in himself the effort of the Indian mind to face the challenge of an age of transition and arrive at a synthesis of the various currents and cross-currents playing upon Indian life. He noticed the effects of British economic policy upon Indian rural economy and put forth his analysis in an outspoken manner through his own journal. He was the first person to go back to the purity of the Vedic and Upanishadic thought in an effort to defend Hinduism against the criticism of Christian missionaries from outside, and the danger of its being debased by superstitions and ritualistic practices from within. As a social reformer, he pleaded for the abolition of caste distinctions and the *sati*. He founded educational institutions and became the first head of the Brahmo Samaj. It is important to look at the life of Raja Rammohun Roy as the life of a man who represented an epoch.

The religious and social reform activities that Roy began took root and set the pattern for similar activities in other parts of the country for nearly half a century to follow. In Bengal itself he was succeeded in this movement by such personalities as Dwarkanath Tagore, Devendranath Tagore and Keshab Chandra Sen. Under Keshab Chandra Sen, the Samajists were engaged in social work activities, such as famine relief, the founding of educational institutions for girls, the emancipation of women, and the encouraging of the movement for temperance and charity. Keshab Chandra Sen had also played a part in the enactment of the Civil Marriage Act of 1872.

In the western part of the country—in Bombay and in Maharashtra particularly—the same religious and social reform movements were agitating the life of the people. In 1949 the Maharashtra Paramhansa Sabha was established and it fought for caste reform. In 1861 Justice Ranade collaborated in the establishment of the Widow Marriage Association. In 1870 he helped in the founding of the Sarvajanik Sabha. In 1882 the

Indian Christian missionary, Pandita Ramabhai, established the Arya Mahila Samaj. The organization of specific social work institutions was undertaken by Jyotiba Phule, a non-Brahmin worker. He established orphanages and schools for girls. The counterpart of the Brahmo Samaj, the Prarthana Samaj, was established in Bombay by Dr Bhandarkar and Justice Ranade.

Other Reform Movements

During this period similar ideas in the field of social reform were being expressed and popularized by the Muslim reformer, Sir Syed Ahmed Khan. He was a writer, an educationist and a social reformer. He founded an educational institution in 1875, which later developed into the Aligarh University, and spent his long and useful life in the promotion of a philosophy which was influenced by the liberal and democratic traditions of the West. In 1885 the opponents of Sir Syed Ahmed Khan founded the Anjuman-i-Himayat-i-Islam in Lahore.

It should be clear from the above that the leaders of public opinion of the nineteenth century were people who had been influenced by Western liberal thought and were, at the same time, conscious of the challenge which this new way of thinking constituted to the customary, religious and social habits of the people. In their efforts, therefore, we see an attempt to show that pure Hinduism on pure Islam did not suffer from the blemishes which were found in the then current practices. Their argument was essentially to the effect that their respective religions were fundamentally right and what was required was only the shedding of the extraneous impurities that had entered into the social life of the people. From this point of view, the social reform activity was also partly a defensive reaction against the onslaught of a foreign religion and culture. This defence took two or three different forms. The Brahmo Samaj was characterized by a genuine appreciation of the principle of God and the abolition of image worship. The members of the movement attempted to organize their lives on a rational basis. They made it a point to discard all superstitions and practices that could not be given a rational explanation. In this emphasis on reason, the Brahmo Samaj could be said to have incorporated the crucially significant element of nineteenth-century progressive thinking.

The Arya Samaj (founded in 1875), which also gave up image worship and abolished the sub-castes, did not succeed in assimilating rationalism as a part of its way of life. The activities of the Samaj were largely motivated by the desire to counteract the Christian missionaries. In this aspect of its work the Samaj became militantly active. The narrowness of this negative approach was, however, partly compensated by the great services that the Samajists rendered in the spread of education in North India.

Unlike the founders of the Brahmo Samaj and the Arya Samaj, the life of Ramakrishna could not be said to be motivated by the desire to purify Hinduism or to defend it against Christianity. It had its own independent inspiration in a mystic experience, but the work of the Ramakrishna Mission, which was founded in 1897 by Swami Vivekananda, was very greatly influenced by the organizational pattern of the Christian missions. To a much greater extent than in the case of the Brahmo Samaj or the Arya Samaj, service became a major part of the function of the Ramakrishna Mission.

The atmosphere of religious questioning and spiritual unrest and the broadening of outlook fostered by liberal teaching were greatly favourable to the successful organization of the Theosophical movement in India. Mrs Besant came to India in 1893 and with her close study, magnetic personality, and persuasive eloquence, succeeded in interesting a large part of the intelligentsia of the country in the Theosophical movement which she headed. Theosophy does not, however, seem to have emphasized the organization of social services to the same extent as the other religious movements of the period had done.

Nineteenth-Century Reform Movements

A quick review of the nineteenth-century reform activity is bound to be incomplete. We may, however, note here two of the broader characteristics:

1. These movements were, as a rule, activated by a religious inspiration. Even if they were not defensive in their origin, their appeal to the people lay largely in the fact that they made it possible for the people to accept new values and patterns of life without loss of pride in their ancient culture.
2. The subjects that engaged the minds of the reformers most were: religion, status of women and their right to property and education, abolition of caste, raising the age of marriage, promotion of widow remarriage, removal of the blemishes of the joint family system, etc.

But even in the nineteenth century, particularly during the last two decades, an entirely different tradition was being established by a new band of social reformers in the four corners of the country. This was a non-religious, liberal tradition. Its leaders were Bhandarkar, Kolhatkar, Chintamani, S. Subramanya Iyer, K. Veeresalingam Pantulu, Narendra Nath Sen, Lala Baij Nath, Ram Kali Chaudhari, and others. They did not seek justification for their views in the *Shastras*; they often attacked them and spoke on the basis of their intellectual convictions. They did not form themselves into a corporate body, but only met annually for about fourteen years, during 1880–1900, in "social conferences". A study of their writings and speeches shows that they were agitated over the same questions as above, but their standpoint was different. They were all individually—with some exceptions—men of faith and belief, but the critical tradition that they established was primarily an intellectual one. This tradition, however, was different from the one that Gokhale and his colleagues were to establish. It was an intellectual tradition, oriented to philosophic generalizations rather than to analysis based on facts.

The religious motivation in social work continued to be operative through the nineteenth century and is still, in a sense, an important factor in the field. Yet, growingly, the rationalistic-humanistic tradition came to be established as an independent force from the beginning of the twentieth century. Among leaders of public opinion in Maharashtra, who pleaded for reform on the basis of reason and without appeal to religious sentiment, the name of Gopal Ganesh Agarkar must stand pre-eminent. He sacrificed popularity and even goodwill in his efforts to establish reason as a motivating factor in personal and social life. He did not gain an immediate following, but his life and writings, his intellectual honesty, and his courage of conviction left a great impress on the thoughtful minds of the next two generations.

The Rationalistic-Humanistic Tradition

Among the many whom Agarkar must have influenced was Gopal Krishna Gokhale. Gokhale was a rationalist but a believer. He embodied the same earnestness of spirit and courage of conviction as Agarkar but his mind was oriented towards political as well as social reform and social work activity. He began his career as an educationist and a co-founder of the Deccan Education Society. He broke away from his colleague, Bal Gangadhar Tilak, because of differences in their approaches to political problems. Gokhale was a moderate and a liberal in the best sense of the term. He was, however, to come to be known more as a social reformer than as a political worker. He founded the Servants of India Society in 1905. This was probably the first major organization in the field of social work, which did not have a religious basis. It was a non-religious organization dedicated to the service of India. It attracted to its fold the best liberal minds of a whole generation. Among its members were to be counted G.K. Deodhar, N.M. Joshi, V. Srinivasa Sastri and H.N. Kunzru.

The peculiar contribution of this early twentieth-century group of social reformers lay in the fact that, irrespective of their personal beliefs, their analysis and argument for social reform activity were based on grounds of reason. They established a tradition of collection and presentation of data and of attempting to argue for reform on the basis of facts. Gokhale and his colleagues insisted on a scholarly study of the problems for which they sought solution. Their public speeches and the memoranda that they submitted to responsible organizations and bodies were, as a rule, closely argued documents. They thus paved the way for a rational and scientific (if not professional) approach to the solution of social problems.

It was obvious that a tradition so strongly intellectual could not expect to gain mass appeal. Its plea for reform reached only the newspaper-reading intelligentsia. It did not succeed in reaching the large number of illiterate men and women whose pattern of life was sought to be reformed.

Another reason for the Servants of India Society and other social work organizations of the early twentieth century failing to become major movements was the preoccupation of the people with the growing nationalist movement. The breach between Gokhale and Tilak was significant. Tilak gave priority to political independence from the British as against internal social reform. In this he received the backing of a large majority of the educated section of the community. And from then on up to 1947 it was the political leader who occupied the position of pre-eminence. The talk of opposition, resistance and rebellion appealed to the frustrated middle classes of the post-First World War era more strongly than the conciliatory attitude of the reformer who was inevitably a moderate.

Gandhi's Contribution

In the context of the development of social reform activity, outlined above, the almost unanimous support that Gandhi received on his appearance in Indian public life in 1920 is easily understandable. His multi-faced personality gave continuity to the religious-rational as well as the politically rebellious trends in our public life.

We of this age have been too closely under the influence of Gandhi to be able to make an objective analysis of the great appeal he had for the people. In a very real sense he made us respect ourselves and stand up as men after centuries of foreign rule. This in itself was a stupendous task, but in accomplishing this he exercised to the maximum his faculties as a man of deep spiritual and religious feeling, a soft-spoken but uncompromising fighter for the country's freedom, and a man of vision regarding the total pattern of life that he wanted to evolve in the country. In his vision, the social, the religious, the political, and the economic did not appear as different aspects. He made a synthetic approach to the problems of life and his activities showed concern and sensitivity to the subtler social and psychological crises through which the country was passing, as also to the more immediate and more material problems in the political and economic life of the country.

It is difficult to write separately about Gandhi's social work and social reform activities. They were a part of his larger public life and were integrated with it. What he called the "constructive programme" was simultaneously a movement for economic betterment and for improving the tenor of social life.

Gandhi pleaded for the equality of women. He believed in it and afforded them that status in his public as well as private life. For the first time in modern Indian history, women stood side by side with men and fought for their country. He did not, however, speak of the rights of women as such. He spoke rather of the duties of men and women. This was characteristic of his whole approach to social problems. He fought and staked his life for a better deal for the Harijans, but he never talked of the rights of Harijans so much as of the duties of the higher castes towards the Harijans. In a sense this approach seemed to encourage a feudal, paternalistic attitude on the part of the higher castes and yet it was a matter of strong faith with him that emphasis on rights divides men whereas emphasis on duties unites them.

As a worker for Harijan welfare Gandhi established the Harijan Sewak Sangh. This body, as will be seen later, worked for the social, economic and political betterment of the Harijans. Gandhi also founded the All-India Village Industries Association which was primarily an organization for the revival of cottage industries and the betterment of rural economic life. But, as a part of his constructive programme, it was also an instrument for the improvement of total human life rather than just its economic aspect. Gandhi established the Nai Talim

Sangh and argued in favour of a system of education geared to the work and life of the people. He was also interested in problems of health and sanitation and his special concern for the lepers was symbolic of his sensitivity to the need for a more enlightened attitude to this problem.

But Gandhi's influence cannot be gauged in terms of the institutions he directly founded or supported. It is to be appreciated more in terms of the basic changes he introduced in our mode of thinking and living, which in their turn were responsible for the many smaller and localized social reform movements that were started. It is in this sense that we can talk of the twentieth century as the age of Gandhi in India. The positive aspects of this influence are obvious. It brought enlightenment to the common man, made him aware of his social as well as economic responsibilities and problems, and made us all think in a fundamental manner on many issues that we face. Gandhi was not concerned with the details of the manner in which the village industries could be revived, or the status of the Harijans could be improved, or a new system of education established. His concern was with the fundamental approach to these questions. The positive aspects of this influence can also be measured in terms of the great strides that the people of India took in regard to these questions that had been agitating the minds of the social and religious reformers.

But the secret of this influence lay in its appeal to the heart rather than to the mind. This is not to deny the clarity with which Gandhi argued every position that he took, but only to reaffirm that his leadership in the social as well as the political field was essentially of a charismatic character. Its strength lay in the emotions it stirred rather than in the analysis with which it was supported.

From this point of view, it is doubtful whether Gandhi strengthened the intellectual tradition of his *guru,* Gokhale. The Servants of India Society had attempted to combine a rational, analytical approach to social problems with the self-denial of a missionary. Gandhi emphasized self-denial in service; he never denied the role of the intellect, but he did not espouse it. The continuity of the intellectual tradition in social work is to be sought in another development, viz., the organization of training for social work.

Preparation for Social Service

The practice of a careful preparation of individuals for a life of social service has existed from ancient times. The form which this preparation took was one of apprenticeship. All missions insist on a new initiate being apprenticed to a senior priest or *swami* for a considerable length of time before he launches on his own. But, as is true of education in general, formal education in social work consisting of a course of lectures and opportunities for supervised work is a recent development. It began in India in the form of a short training course organized by the Social Service League in Bombay in the 1920s. This was a significant development. It meant a departure from the notion that one who wanted to help need only go out and do it. The courses were meant for young men and women who wanted to offer their voluntary services for social work. There was no idea of training for paid positions or for a profession. This would have been considered a mercenary motive.

Therefore, when Sir Dorabji Tata Graduate School of Social Work was established in 1936 for preparing students for the profession of social work, it made a major departure from the established traditions in the country. "Social work" was a term synonymous with voluntariness. Individual agencies had paid employees, but they were not called social workers. Even professional social work does not view all paid employees of service agencies as social workers. The term signifies a certain field of activity and the utilization of certain skills. From this viewpoint not even persons who work voluntarily need all be called social workers. There are persons who work voluntarily and are politicians; there are others who work voluntarily and are members of the judiciary; there are still others who are doctors, nurses and educationists. It is possible to conceive of people from almost any field of activity who would render voluntary services; this act of voluntariness does not make them social workers from the professional standpoint. In this view social work implies the practice of certain skills in the area of social welfare. Any one, paid or voluntary, who practises them is a social worker. These skills, in professional jargon, are listed as Case Work, Group Work, and Community Organization.

Place of Professional Social Work

The profession of social work has its origin in fellow feeling and a desire to be of help to others, but its moorings are in social science. Social sciences have helped change the entire approach to social problems. We have moved in emphasis from punishment to rehabilitation, from amelioration to prevention. The principles of science are designed to inculcate an attitude of questioning rather than dogmatism. The good professional masters his techniques without being limited by them.

But professional social workers, however well-equipped, cannot be substituted for the lay-leader. They are not cast in the heroic mould of a Raja Rammohun Roy, or a Gokhale, or a Gandhi. They are humbler men who have a certain equipment of knowledge and skills to handle problems of institutional management and interpersonal and inter-group relations. At worst they are men and women doing a job only to earn a living; at best they are persons with a sense of social purpose and pride of the profession to which they belong. At present, their weakness lies in a lack of the fervour and the drive that comes from emotional conviction; their strength should lie in a widened perspective and a capacity to work methodically and dispassionately. Being paid for their work they are only in a position to do efficiently a job that, a community feels, needs to be done; but they cannot easily move a community to accept wholly new ideas which affect its value system. They cannot, in this sense, become pioneers and leaders of movements; they cannot gain the moral right to preach to or to admonish a group. But for the same reason, they are free from a sense of martyrdom and sacrifice which in lesser men makes it impossible for them to help without hurting.

The professional social workers are, however, a very small group in the country. They are yet a very young group. The oldest among them have not been in the field for more than about eighteen years. But they are a growing group. There may be doubts and questions about the adequacy and suitability of the particular training they are receiving now, but the idea of professional training, as such, has come to stay.

New Trends in Social Work

From the point of view of the development of thought in the field of social reform and social work the account given above brings us up to the present period. The only significant new happening in this area during the past few years has been the considerable increase in state social welfare activity. This has primarily been occasioned by the size and nature of the problem of the rehabilitation of displaced persons that our central and state governments have had to tackle since independence. There is also the constitution of the Employees' State Insurance Corporation. Significant for voluntary social services is also the constitution of the Central Social Welfare Board. Finally, of the greatest potential significance is the constitution of a Division of Social Security in the Central Government. But more of this later.

Types of Welfare Institutions

In an effort to find out whether any specific trend could be discovered in the type of social work institutions organized during the period under review, the author attempted to analyze the directories of the social service agencies for three of the major cities of India, viz., Bombay, Calcutta and Madras. The attempt was to find out whether we could say that in the organization of social work institutions child welfare preceded welfare of women which, in its own turn, preceded some other types of institutions. There are obvious limitations in undertaking such studies on the basis of directories of existing institutions. It is clear that these directories would not list the names of institutions which were founded at one time, but exist no longer, yet for the purpose of our interest such institutions which no longer exist are of equal, and perhaps even greater, importance than the ones that exist. But since no other data are immediately available, the listings in the directories were used as a basis.

It seems that child welfare has been one of the oldest fields of social work in the modern Indian period. Charity schools and orphanages were established as early as the eighteenth century. The specific care of physically handicapped children, however, assumed importance much later. By the end of the nineteenth century, we find that institutions for the deaf and mute had been founded. Another field which enlisted public interest early enough was the organization of charitable hospital services. We find that some of these hospitals financed primarily by private funds were organized in the middle of the nineteenth century. The end of the nineteenth century shows the beginning of the organization of charities and trusts. Quite a number of these trusts were organized for individual communities and sects. During the same period we find the beginnings of the organization of education societies. This is also the period of the formation of communal and regional reform associations. The first decade of the twentieth century is only a continuation of the same trends. The second and third decades, however, are marked by the initiation and growth of activities in the field of women's welfare. The period after 1930 is marked by the development of the concept of constructive work, Harijan welfare and adult education. As already indicated, these remarks are of a very general character and need to be further substantiated by closer studies.

Co-ordination in Welfare Work

During the two centuries of growth of organized social services a large number of voluntary social service agencies have grown and today it is estimated that there are about ten thousand such agencies spread through the length and breadth of the country. Most of these agencies are in the urban areas, large metropolitan cities, middle-sized district headquarters, and small towns. Very few of them are organized by rural folk to serve the rural areas. With this growth in organized social services a need is being felt for more information about these agencies, their potentialities and problems. It has become necessary also to provide for greater communication and exchange of information between these agencies so that a more harmonized pattern of services can develop. In response to these needs a new trend for the organization of co-ordinating bodies is to be detected. There is the Indian Adult Education Association which seeks to co-ordinate the activities of organizations in the field of adult and social education. There is the Indian Conference of Social Work which has for its purpose the co-ordination of the activities of organization in the broader field of social work and social welfare. Recently, the Indian Council for Child Welfare has been organized with a view to effect co-ordination among child welfare organizations. Though all these organizations have been brought into existence for purposes of co-ordination, most of them are called upon to initiate new activities and to organize their own regional bodies, so that the work of co-ordination on the regional level could be effectively undertaken. Recently, views have been expressed that there is a place for co-ordinating bodies in the field of youth welfare and rural welfare.

The work of most of these co-ordinating organizations is hampered by the paucity of funds. The work that they desire to undertake cannot have the same appeal to humanitarian sentiments as the direct social welfare activities in the field are likely to have. The work consists of research, organization of conferences, publication of journals, etc. The validity of work of this nature is not commonly recognized and these bodies have often to go from one government department to another to seek financial aid for their programmes.

There are also certain intrinsic difficulties in the way of co-ordination. To the extent that co-ordination is limited to exchange of information and views, there are no serious obstacles in its way, but as soon as co-ordination is interpreted to mean the surrender of a part of the autonomy of individual institutions difficulties arise. It is, in no small measure, due to problems of this nature that co-ordinating organizations have generally not proceeded beyond the stage of exchange of information and organization of conferences. This is so not only in our country but also in other countries where the organization of institutionalized service has had a longer history.

With this we come to the end of the first section of the chapter, which seeks to trace the development of social thought in the fields of social reform and welfare. The author has also tried to show the relationship between this particular development and the general trends in the social thought of the period.

There is, however, another aspect of the growth and development of social work which has not been dealt with either in the pages preceding nor again specifically in the pages to follow. This aspect relates to the role that state agencies have played, or are playing, in the institution of the many welfare services that are organized in the country. The subject is obviously too broad to be adequately covered in a few pages. And yet an outline, however sketchy it may be, will serve a useful purpose in giving the reader a bird's eye view of state activity in the welfare field. Such an attempt is made in the following paragraphs.

Concept of State Responsibility for Social Welfare

The concept that there is an obligation upon the state to ensure the well-being of the citizen is a very recent one in human history though through varied forms of religious and secular charity the community and even the state has always sought to provide for the care and maintenance of the poor. In Britain the government took direct cognizance of the problems of the poor in 1536 when the first Poor Law was enacted. This was amended and consolidated during the reign of Queen Elizabeth I between 1597 and 1601. This Act defined the scope of state interest in the area of social welfare for well over two hundred years. Even in the nineteenth century when this Act was further amended there was no general acceptance of the proposition that the government should make itself responsible for the individual welfare of its citizens. It was only in the twentieth century, and then between the two world wars that a major change in attitudes took place and the goal of a welfare state—as different from a state governed by the principle of lassez-faire—came to be popularly accepted. Today, particularly since the Second World War, the government in Britain, and nearly in all industrially advanced countries, takes responsibility for a wide variety of services to meet the problems of ill-health, ignorance, economic dependence, physical handicap, social disability, and mental illness or retardation. The stigma of pauperism is no longer attached to the condition of being needy or to the acceptance of a service intended to meet that need.

In India, the state has not so far assumed direct or complete responsibility for the provision of welfare services to all its citizens. During the pre-British as well as the British period this responsibility lay largely on voluntary charitable agencies though the state did offer direct assistance to the citizens during famines and other emergencies. In the post-independence period the country has accepted the goal of a welfare state wherein the state shall, within the limits of its economic capacity, make effective provision for securing the right to work, education, and public assistance in all cases of undeserved want. So far, the government has found the economic capacity of the state far too inadequate to enable it to accept the responsibilities listed in this directive principle of state policy.

On the other hand, within the limits set by the available economic resources, the government has sought to pursue the implications of this state policy. In the pursuit of its goal the government has distinguished between the social service needs of the general population, the special needs of large groups or classes of people who have traditionally suffered social disabilities—as in the case of the Scheduled Castes, the Scheduled Tribes, and Other Backward Classes—and the special needs of individual citizens who may be handicapped because of a special circumstance. Apart from the developments in the fields of health and education, which are grouped as a part of social services and distinguished from welfare services, the acceptance of the goal to meet all situations of undeserved want has led to a considerable expansion of welfare services organized directly through statutory agencies as well as indirectly through voluntary and aided agencies to assist persons in the latter two categories. The following paragraphs will provide a brief, and necessarily hurried, review of the major services developed in these areas.

Some Social and Welfare Services Offered by the State

Social Services

In education the most important single achievement has been the expansion in the facilities for primary education. In 1950 only 42 per cent of the children in the age group 6–11 years were in school, by 1960 this percentage has increased to 63, and it is expected that by 1966 all the children of school-going age will be in schools. The number of high schools, colleges, and institutions of higher learning has also nearly doubled. But in education the problem is not only one of physical facilities and their quantitative increase. Even more important is the availability of qualified and experienced teachers and the building of sound methods of education. This is the bottleneck in most planning for educational development. No adequate methods have yet been found to meet these urgent needs despite the increase in teacher training institutions.

One of the major efforts in the field of health has been to extend the benefit of health services in rural areas. While one cannot say that today medical assistance, or even protected supply of pure water, is available in all the villages, the establishment of over 3,000 Primary Health Centres has certainly brought much-needed assistance to many of the villages. Each of these centres is supposed to serve all the villages in a development block. It is obvious that a centre cannot effectively serve such a large number of widely dispersed communities.

The significance of this new development lies in that a new agency has been conceived which looks at the problem of health from all its varied angles. The centre provides public health education, supervises the preventive health services, and offers through its team a variety of medical services.

Another programme initiated by the Ministry of Health and presently restricted to the employees of the Central Government is the Contributory Health Service Scheme which offers comprehensive health insurance to its members. Much valuable experience can be gained through the operation of this scheme which will be useful if the service is extended in due course to other sections of the population. Another large group which benefits by a similar facility is made up of industrial workers who are covered by the Employees' State Insurance Scheme.

Two other programmes in the field of health are of special interest to welfare workers. One of these is the programme of family planning. India is one of the few countries which have adopted population control through varied measures of family planning as a deliberate policy. A Family Planning Board has been established to direct the work in this sphere. Over 3,500 clinics have been established in different parts of the country, which advise on family planning matters and supply equipment to those in need. Campaigns for vasectomy and sterilization have been conducted and generally a fair degree of awareness of the need for family planning has been created.

Finally, there is the nutritional programme of mid-day meals for school children. This is a programme still in its initial stages. It is being selectively operated in a few areas in some seven or eight states. The programme depends largely on milk and food stuffs received as aid from abroad.

Welfare of Backward Classes

In the case of backward classes the state has a special responsibility to provide for their welfare and development. Backward classes are made up of Scheduled Castes (SCs), Scheduled

Tribes (STs), Denotified Communities and the Other Backward Classes (OBCs). Of these, the first three groups are clearly identified and listed. They are also groups which stand in special need of protection as well as assistance. For SCs and STs the government seeks to provide special opportunity for advancement through reservations in legislatures and in posts under the government and through various social and economic measures of assistance, such as scholarships, reservations in schools and colleges, loans for occupational purposes, housing facilities, hostels, etc. Most of these facilities, except reservation in legislatures, are variously made available to members of OBCs too in different states. In the case of the SCs a special protective law called the Untouchability Offences Act was passed by parliament.

The various measures have been helpful in promoting the growth of educational and other services in scheduled (tribal) areas as well as among the members of SCs. One cannot, however, say that we have achieved either the total removal of untouchability or any tangible progress in the economic condition of the tribal populations. In a way it is erroneous to expect that such progress can be achieved by this compartmental approach. While SCs and STs are undoubtedly at special disadvantage in comparison with other communities and need to be given additional opportunities, their progress cannot be achieved independent of the extent of progress in the rest of the society.

This is specially true of the category OBCs. Many of the state governments have seen the futility of identifying these groups by means of caste criteria and some of them have moved to the adoption of economic criteria for determining the eligibility of individuals for benefits conferred by the government. The acceptance of economic and other objective criteria for affording relief might be one way of converting this scheme of special benefits into an incipient programme of public assistance. The government, however, is not in a position to accept the economic implications of such a decision, however rational it might be. The problem is one of creating new resources—for jobs as for everything else—and not merely of distributing these resources more equitably. In the meantime, the government finds it necessary to resort to the criterion of caste affiliation both on grounds of equity and of political expediency.

Social Welfare Services

The service subsumed under the title "social welfare" have been many and varied. They have often been grouped in the following categories: child welfare, women's welfare, welfare of the physically and mentally handicapped, welfare of the slum dwellers and social defence.

One of the common characteristics of services in all these different fields has been that, with the exception of social defence services, most of the others are organized largely by voluntary agencies and are conceived of in an ad hoc fashion. There is no concept of any national or regional goals which are sought to be achieved.

In the field of child welfare, a great deal of emphasis has been laid on the programme of pre-school education in rural as well as urban areas. The number of *Balvadis* established during the Second and the Third Plans runs into more than a few thousand. Yet there is no rationale given of why these programmes are being undertaken and what proportion or what sections of the population we seek to reach through this service in the foreseeable future. When there is no immediate possibility of achieving national coverage, administrators tend to apply the terms "experimental" or "demonstration" or "pilot" to the projects which are launched on an entirely ad hoc basis.

This does not mean that *Balvadis* do not provide a meaningful programme. There is probably a special justification for providing such institutionalized pre-school facilities for certain sections of the population. But which sections? It is obvious that with the difficulties we have in providing universal primary school education—and this is a constitutional obligation—there is little likelihood of providing universal pre-school education. Then, why this ad hoc programme of hundreds and thousands of Balvadis?

In the sphere of women's welfare, some of the important programmes have been those of welfare extension projects for rural women, social-economic schemes and hostels for working women. Today, there are about a thousand extension projects and close to one hundred hostels. For none of these programmes, however, are there any definite targets worked out on a long-term basis. Is there going to be one welfare extension project per block? How many socio-economic projects would we need if we have to create additional income opportunities for a sizeable number of women? Even in the provision of hostels—which should be a project limited only to large industrial areas—there is no idea of achieving relative adequacy in the context of assessed needs.

In the case of the socially dependent persons the major responsibility has been taken by voluntary agencies and their chief method of tackling the problem has been institutional care. There is no exact estimate of the number of such institutions caring for unattached women, destitutes and orphaned children. Most of these institutions, unless they are denominational, receive assistance from public funds.

The care of the physically handicapped was also largely an area of voluntary effort. In recent years the central and state governments have taken a more direct part in organizing some of these service, particularly in the areas of the training of teachers and the training of handicapped adults. It is obvious that these institutions meet only a fraction of the total population. Recently, more emphasis has been laid on the need to serve the handicapped in the community itself and it is suggested that in large urban areas it might be possible to organize the schooling of blind children in the schools for the visually normal. Another service initiated for the physically handicapped relates to their occupational rehabilitation. Through special employment officers efforts are made to find suitable placements for handicapped but occupationally trained persons in industry.

The social defence services are primarily made up of service for the juvenile delinquents, the beggars, and women in moral danger. These services are very unevenly developed in different parts of the country though in many cases they constitute the direct responsibility of the respective state governments. Some of the states have not enacted appropriate laws in respect of these persons and in others even after the laws have been passed their enforcement is postponed or limited to particular areas. However, it may be generally said that the more industrialized states have tended to adopt these laws and enforce them at least in their major urban areas.

Need for a Middle-range Policy in Social Welfare

If the state has been unable to ensure adequate coverage in its social services and services for the backward classes because of economic limitations, these limitations have equally hampered the systematic development of welfare services. It is clear that today the government has little funds to establish a comprehensive system of social security whereby all situations of "undeserved want" would be provided for. But there has not even been an effort to define carefully the immediate and middle-range objectives in social welfare from which to work gradually for broader and broader coverage. Despite the efforts of successive working groups appointed in preparation for each plan, most activity in the field of social welfare continues to be of an ad hoc nature.

An important reason for this situation is that in practice as well as in principle the government has regarded this as an area where voluntary agencies should be primarily responsible. This decision is governed as much by the considerations of expediency as of deliberate policy. Since the government cannot itself provide all the services, they emphasize the special contribution that can be made by voluntary endeavour. While no one can deny the important role that voluntary sector can or should play in social welfare, this can hardly be the argument for absolving the state of its legitimate responsibility. Besides, even while voluntary agencies are encouraged to undertake welfare activities, the state must set down the outline of an overall plan which can be seen as leading systematically to the goal of universal coverage.

In conformity with the policy of encouraging voluntary agencies in the social welfare field, the Central Government has instituted a grant-giving programme through the Central Social Welfare Board. Apart from this, the state governments and municipal bodies have their own programmes of grants-in-aid to voluntary bodies. There is no estimate readily available of the total funds expended by these different statutory agencies. The Central Social Welfare Board began with a relatively small allocation of Rs 40 million during the First Plan and has by now more than trebled this figure. The chances are that this allocation will be sought to be nearly doubled in the Fourth Plan. It has already aided over ten thousand different agencies.

A massive grants-in-aid programme can be an instrument for ensuring satisfactory standards in the organization of services and for ensuring general conformity to an overall plan of development. This has not yet happened to the extent one would wish. The Board could by itself work on raising the adequacy of standards, but it is hardly in a position to ensure planned development, unless there is already a plan. As indicated earlier, the outline of an overall plan in social welfare development has not yet been evolved or even attempted.

One factor responsible for this position was the absence of any group or agency in government which considered social welfare as its main, special and continuing responsibility. The various areas of social welfare have traditionally been divided among several ministries and no ministry thought it necessary to think beyond its particular concern. It is only now in the middle of 1964 that a new Division of Social Security has been created in the Ministry of Law and Social Security, wherein all subjects with a welfare orientation—that were formerly divided among the Ministries of Health, Home, Labour and Education—have been brought together. This is indeed one of the most significant developments that have taken place in the social welfare field since independence. One expects many things from such a development, but minimally what one hopes for is that it will give rise to co-ordinated programmes in social welfare or to the evolution of an overall, long-term policy relating to the areas of social welfare, the welfare of backward classes and social security.

CHAPTER THREE

THE APPROACH IN CHILD WELFARE

The twentieth century has been called the "Century of the Child" and the nations of the world seem to have become suddenly aware of the problems and the great potentialities of childhood. It is true that childhood and children have always been the subjects of much romanticizing in all literature. In Sanskrit poetry, children have been referred to as the jewels of the home. Poets through the ages have sung about the innocence and purity of childhood; they have compared children to flowers, to stars, to birds, and to all objects with which are associated our ideas of beauty, delicacy and softness. It is also true that orphaned children, homeless children and children in difficulty have always moved the conscience of the community to action in all countries.

Yet there is a sense in which it would be specially appropriate to refer to the present century as the Century of the Child. Never before had the needs of children stood in the danger of being completely overlooked, their simple nature being misguided, and their helplessness being exploited as at the beginning of the industrial age. The industrial age brought changes not only in work-life, but also in home-life. The place of work became separated from the place of living. This meant also a separation between the man and his family and sometimes even between parents and their children. When

---

Paper read before a seminar convened by the Indian Council of Child Welfare, Bihar State Branch, at Patna in 1956.

therefore the children were not working beyond their strength inside a factory, they would be wandering aimlessly through the lanes and back-alleys of the new industrial township. The close-knit, small community of the village was no longer there to exercise a wholesome control. Its place had been taken by the impersonal proximity of city dwellers who called themselves neighbours because the lived in adjoining houses. The frustrations of slum life, the unguided conditions of childhood, the contrasts and the temptations of urban living, the weakening of the authority of elders, and the unhealthy surroundings of early industrial townships gave rise to the types of problems which had not been experienced before. Children suffered not only because of their own mistakes and follies but also because of the follies of their parents. The problems of destitution, desertion, unmarried motherhood and broken homes, all contributed to the problems of delinquency, vagrancy, truancy and homelessness among children.

Novelists of the last quarter of the nineteenth century became acutely conscious of the hazards of childhood in the slums of the new cities. The English novelist Charles Dickens was only the most distinguished of them all. The revelations made by these novelists shocked the conscience of the people. They created an atmosphere favourable for the growth of social service activity aimed at mitigating the evils to which children were exposed. The great social workers at the end of the last century devoted themselves to meeting the challenge of the city slums. It was not till the twentieth century, however, that the urge to give all children a fair chance in life became a real movement.

In a large measure this development must be attributed to the growth of psychology and the social sciences. Psychology in particular came forth with theories which were as momentous in their impact as they were shocking to our orthodox sensibilities. It gave an insight into the dynamic process by which our minds grow and our personalities develop. Its contributions helped in the treatment of mental diseases where the ideas of custody and physical torture were replaced with understanding, analysis and clinical guidance. It changed our ideas of child rearing in the family where, despite the poetic imagery about sweet childhood, the ruling concept was one of coercive authority in making the child learn to do and not do certain things. It challenged our system of education, with its emphasis on absorption of information and learning by rote, and pointed to one which emphasized development of the thinking process through activity, problem solution and project execution.

These developments had an inevitable effect on the trends in the field of child welfare. It made clear that while the dependent and delinquent child needed to be helped, it was equally important to help in the promotion of the normal growth of children living in their homes and communities. Child welfare activities became more broad-based covering not only the already afflicted but also the still unafflicted.

In fact, the objectives of child welfare became even wider. They were not restricted to preventive goals. More positive objectives of helping the fullest possible growth of the mind, body, and personality of every child irrespective of class, creed, race, or nationality came to be accepted. The fundamental needs of children were listed and charters have now been drawn up incorporating the fundamental rights of children.

Our understanding of the process of child development has deepened. We no longer refer to childhood as necessarily a blissful state. It can be a blissful state for every child if its physical and emotional needs are met. But if they are not, the life of a child can be a continued state of tension and anxiety. In fact, a child suffers much more under these strains than an adult who has developed the ability to manage and control them. The physical needs of a child are simple and easily perceived. The emotional needs are also simple, but not easily perceived. They are commonly listed as the seven fundamental needs of every child—the need for affection, for physical and emotional security, for being accepted as an individual, for self-respect, for achievement, etc. The simplicity of these needs, however, should not make us lose sight of their crucial significance. The non-satisfaction of these needs means frustration which in its own turn would have consequences that would vary in their gravity depending upon a number of other factors characterizing the life-situation of the child.

The ability of the parents to meet these needs of their children is much dependent upon their own personalities. It used to be considered enough for a parent to be fond of his child for him to be able to look after his child. Now, we know that fondness or love is not enough; it is important to know how to love your child wisely. A possessing, doting love can be injurious to the growth of a child's personality. Over-protection and rejection of a child on the part of the parent can both be equally harmful for the child's personality growth.

While frustrations are painful, they are also an inevitable part of the life of every person. The growing child has also to be helped to accept the limitations of life around him and to manage his frustrations. It is only thus that he becomes equipped to meet such situations in adult life. This approach to understanding a child's insistent demand for a particular object has completely changed our approach to physical punishment. Physical punishment is considered largely unnecessary. It is felt that a parent who can be consistent in his dealings with the child and can be firm on his do's and don'ts without finding the need to punish or bribe the child into acquiescence will really be able to help his child grow normally without unnecessary anxieties. It is not the denial of an object so much as the inconsistent attitude of the parents regarding whether he should or should not have it that is harmful for a child.

The insight of the poet who said "child is the father of man" has been substantially borne out by modern psychological studies. It is during childhood that the foundations of the personality of an individual are laid. If we want a generation of thinking, courageous, democratic, socially responsible citizens, we will have to begin rearing them in our nurseries, schools and playgrounds. What is more we will not succeed in rearing such a generation except to the extent that we ourselves can think and act in consonance with the expectations of the future generation. The role of parents is therefore a very crucial one and a vigorous child welfare movement will have to devote itself to bringing home to our parents the responsibilities of this role.

If the role that the parents play in the growth of a child's personality is an important one so is the role of the teacher. The new teacher will not depend upon the use of the rod to make the child learn his lessons. In fact, the very concept of learning has changed. Learning is a by-product of acting, thinking and experiencing. The new teacher, especially the teacher of very young children, therefore, concentrates on giving the child the opportunities to do and think in a meaningful manner. Children are not to be coerced into learning. Learning should result as naturally as the physical growth of the child.

Play and recreation are not to be frowned upon as so much wasteful activity, but are to be looked upon as necessary and wholesome. Play is now seen to have a great variety of significance. In the first place it is an activity enjoyable in itself and in so far as it is enjoyable it need not require justification on any other grounds. But play can also become a medium through which the child works out his anxieties and worries. In this sense it has therapeutic value. It is also a way in which the child learns to co-ordinate the muscles of the body, to meet problematic situations, and solve them. For a slightly higher age group, play is one of the best media for promotion of the social growth of the child. The attitudes of co-operation, team spirit, healthy rivalry, sportsmanship can all be developed through properly guided play activity. A healthy children's movement will therefore utilize the immense potentialities of organized recreational activity for aiding the growth of children—physically, mentally and socially.

The new insight that science has given us into the process of child growth and development has thus necessitated a re-orientation of our attitudes to child upbringing, education and play. We will now turn to the care of those children who are socially dependent and thus in need of special services. These are the children who have been forsaken, orphaned, destitute, or otherwise without proper guidance and care. Traditionally, our effort has been to put these children in institutions where they are given food and clothing and some smattering of an education and are discharged on their attaining the age of fifteen or sixteen to fend for themselves in the world. Our prime impulse in organizing these services has been pity and sympathy and not a concern for the proper upbringing of these children. If we were concerned with the latter, we would not stop after giving them the bare necessities of life. If children living in families have their emotional needs, so have children living in institutions. In fact, the needs of institutionalized children for emotional support and satisfaction are likely to be greater because they are starved of them. For this reason it is now commonly accepted that even the best-managed institution cannot be a good substitute for a home. The tendency therefore is, wherever possible, to give children in adoption or for foster care.

It is, however, true that the opportunities for adoption and foster-home care are always limited. An attempt is therefore made to approximate the atmosphere of the institution to that of the home by dividing the inmates into small cottage groups where they will be under the care of an elderly person and where they will try to organize life as in a home. Yet, the mere provision of cottages in place of large dormitories is no guarantee that the children will receive the care that they need for their normal growth. Due attention has to be paid to their physical and emotional needs. One major difference between a home and an institution lies in the fact that the child at home is accepted as a distinct individual with his likes and dislikes, with his needs and potentialities. This individualizing of the inmates of an institution is not easy and yet that to a large extent is the secret of a good deal of the emotional satisfaction that a child derives at home. The staff of an institution must be equipped temperamentally and by training to detect the special needs and characteristics of each child and to strive to meet these needs to the extent possible.

With older children the institution has to accept the responsibility for giving proper education in letters and in vocations. Here again, the aptitudes and abilities of children must be studied and they should be given the training most suited to them. The institution must also help a child to develop healthy social attitudes in life. A democratic mode of organization of institutional life in which children share and participate in the responsibilities of the institution can go a long way in helping the children to develop attitudes conducive to a democratic and co-operative pattern of living.

Our responsibilities towards institutionalized children do not cease once we have given them education and vocational training. Even on going out of the institutions they will need help in settling down in their individual lives. For sometime after they have found a job, therefore, we must maintain a friendly interest in the welfare of these children and provide the after-care services that would be needed by them.

Finally, we turn to the delinquent juvenile—the child that comes into conflict with law. Our attitude to the delinquent juvenile used to be the same as our attitude to a delinquent adult—which was one of punishment, custody and retribution. We used to look upon offenders as persons who were incorrigibly depraved and who could be kept out of mischief only be restricting their freedom. Today, offenders are looked upon as maladjusted persons who need to be helped and corrected. We now believe that people commit offences not because of inherited tendencies but because of the influence of a combination of unfavourable factors—environmental as well as personal. This approach shifts the emphasis from punishment and detention to prevention, correction and rehabilitation.

In the case of the juvenile offenders, the plea for a changed attitude and a changed programme is doubly strengthened because a person of young age is also a person who is yet immature and cannot therefore be expected to understand the full implications of his actions. At the same time, he is a person who can yet be guided and re-educated in his habits. If a child is susceptible to bad influences, so is he sensitive to a good environment. The juvenile offender has therefore to be re-educated either in a protected or in an open environment. The whole set of concepts associated with offence, arrest, police investigation and conviction are outmoded in this new context. We have to have probation officers and special juvenile courts which conduct enquiries and recommend appropriate treatment for the child who has probably been misled and misguided.

We thus see that the context within which child welfare activities are to be organized has radically changed as a result of the findings of psychology and the social sciences. A new approach more befitting this "century of the child" has to be evolved.

CHAPTER FOUR

PHILOSOPHY OF SOCIAL WORK

Modern Indian social history begins with the consolidation of British power in the early decades of the nineteenth century, an event marked and facilitated by the final surrender of the Peshwas in 1818. Life in pre-British India was characterized by (i) the close-knit social economy of the caste-cum-community structure of the rural areas with its own compensatory traditional regulations governing inter-community relations, (ii) the co-operative social insurance afforded by the joint family which was at the same time an economic unit for the purposes of production and consumption, and (iii) the panchayat system which dispensed justice with equity.

The British influence brought some changes in the situation. The rural economy was disturbed by the fact that India came to be regarded as the supply depot of raw material for British industries and a ready market for the finished goods. The structure of the joint family was found to be incompatible with the newly introduced forces of industrialization. The caste structure with all its inequities could not be harmonized with the new liberalistic philosophy which came to be professed by the English-educated middle classes. The pantheistic beliefs of popular Hinduism were seriously challenged by

---

Paper submitted to the Fourth Session of the Indian Conference of Social Work (1951) and published in the *Indian Journal of Social Work*, Volume XII (1951–52).

Christianity, and Christianity enjoyed a special prestige as the religion of the ruling caste.

A need for rethinking the values of Indian culture arose. The immediate reaction was defensive. Values were not reconsidered but re-emphasized. The people were reminded by their leaders of the glories of the Vedic period and the days of Asoka, Chandragupta and Akbar. But, the more sensitive minds were self-critical and introspective. They saw the weak spots in India's social structure and the value on which it was founded. At the same time, they were both critical and appreciative of the social, cultural and political influence exerted by the British power.

The foremost of the Indian thinkers of the nineteenth century reflected the crisis that was precipitated by the conflicting currents of thought and beliefs of the age. The intellectual conflict was restricted to the educated classes, but the effects of the basic changes that were being wrought were felt by the masses as well. The writings and the work of Raja Rammohun Roy have a great symbolical significance in the study of this period. He wrote and struggled against the devastating effects of British economic policy on Indian economy. He entered into voluminous arguments through the columns of his newspapers with Christian missionaries, trying to establish the finer spiritual values of Vedic and Upanishadic thought. At the same time, he made a plea with his countrymen for the abolition of caste distinctions and the *sati* system. He established newspapers and educational institutions. And finally to meet the spiritual challenge of Christianity he founded the Brahmo Samaj which did away with image worship and turned to the Upanishads for inspiration and solace.

The mid-nineteenth century saw similar efforts being made in the rest of India. Deshmukh (*alias* Lokahitavadi) wrote his articles analysing the causes of the poverty of the Indian masses. Jyotiba Phule, a non-Brahmin worker, established orphanages and schools for girls and canvassed public opinion in favour of widow remarriage. Dr Bhandarkar and Justice Ranade founded the Prarthana Samaj.

The work of the various Christian missions in India needs to be noted. Even before the nineteenth century the activities of some of the missions had been initiated. By establishing schools and colleges, hospitals and dispensaries, orphanages and foundling homes, leper asylums and blind schools, the missionaries pioneered into new and till then neglected fields of service. A correct appreciation and estimate of their role is a subject for more detailed study. What may be noted here is the fact that despite all the controversy that raged round the activities of the Christian church in India, its missions set a method and pattern of work in this field that was to influence all efforts for a long time to come.

The influence of the church on the spiritual and humanitarian activities of the period is very evident. But coupled with it is the influence of liberalism and rationalism as a philosophy of life. The woman's status in social life becomes a subject of special importance. The need for education is increasingly appreciated.

In the midst of this awakening came into being the Indian National Congress. For a time it seemed to offer a joint platform for social reformers, spiritual leaders and revolutionaries. But more and more the emphasis came to be laid on the economic and political problems. The reformers and spiritual leaders had find to other channels of expression. The rift between Tilak and Agarkar in Poona was symbolical.

Social reform and religious enthusiasm continued together for some time longer. During 1875–95 the Ramakrishna Mission, the Arya Samaj, and the Theosophical Society were founded. The first two bodies were in the nature of religious orders, but as part of their faith they took to service of the needy and the suffering. It is difficult to say whether or not this indicates the influence of Christian missionary activity. But the thought of Ramakrishna incorporated as an integral part of its religious philosophy the virtues of love, charity and service. The Arya Samaj of Dayanand Saraswati opened the possibility of reconversion of Christian and Muslim converts to Hinduism.

In terms of social service the two movements helped by establishing orphanages, widow homes, free dispensaries and relief centres in periods of emergency. The Theosophical movement did not have this social service counterpart. For a time it was closely associated through its leader with the Home Rule League agitation. But later, in this as in other fields, the extremists gained leadership.

In course of time humanitarian ideals came to seek new support in rationalistic principles rather than in religious inclinations. The founding of the Servants of India Society in 1905 is important in that this organization combined the ideal of a devoted life of service with a rational, liberal outlook. Inspired and guided by its members, the Society's activities have not always been directly in the name of the organization itself. Broadly, the cause of education, of co-operation, of labour, of the aboriginals, and of the Harijans gained substantially through the activities of its members.

The various currents of social reform, religious feeling and political aspirations moved largely independent of one another during the period 1903–20. By 1920 Gandhi had come to stay on the Indian scene. He seemed to offer the kind of synthesis the nation wanted, if the inner conflicts were to be avoided. In the imagination of the people he combined within him religious feeling, reformist ardour and revolutionary zeal. Increasingly, in his public life, the religious and the revolutionary seemed to find a more adequate expression. With increased conviction he turned toward the political solution as the first in order of priority. As a result, the cause of immediate social reform and service suffered.

But Gandhi was not blind to the need for such activity. He tried to provide for it through the constructive programme and through the work of such organizations as the Harijan Sevak Sangh, the Gandhi Seva Sangh, etc. Gandhi's approach was not religious; it owed no allegiance to any denomination. Yet it had a spiritual foundation. There was the acceptance of Christian poverty as an ideal for a social worker; there was the emphasis laid on the non-involvement of the ego in the work in hand; there was perhaps an implied acceptance of service as a means to salvation. Its rationale consisted of (i) an intuitive perception of the essential unity of life behind its many facets—when it is shorn of all specialisms, and (ii) the philosophy of democracy at the lowest level made possible by self-sufficiency and decentralization. Its substance was provided formally in the Fourteen-Point Programme enunciated by him.

In the period following upon the death of Gandhi there are indications that the thought pattern analysed above will crystallize into a school. Such a tendency is fraught with danger. However wholesome it might be from the point of view of establishing organizations, it is inimical to the free play of reason. There is a need to re-establish continually the validity of our objectives and the efficacy of our methods.

The late thirties saw the introduction of a new element in the field of social work. The Sir Dorabji Tata Graduate School of Social Work was founded in 1936. In the organization of its courses, it was modelled on the Graduate School of Social Work of USA. Its approach to social work may be adequately described as scientific and professional. Its plea for the acceptance of scientific methods was not perhaps wholly new. The values of science had been appreciated by Swami Vivekananda—the founder of the Ramakrishna Mission—and by the founder and members of the Servants of India Society, who always insisted on a study of facts as a basis for action. The development of specific techniques based on a scientific understanding of social and personal dynamics had, however, never been attempted. Nor could such a development have been felt necessary. Apparently the problems that face a social worker in India have an elemental simplicity. They are mass problems which do not seem to require any subtle analysis. It has always seemed that the solution of the basic problem of our economy would automatically lead to a gradual resolution of all the other intricacies of the situation. This attitude still persists and explains the scant attention that social welfare has received at the hands of our planners.

At the same time, the Tata Institute of Social Sciences—the present name of the Sir Dorabji Tata Graduate School of Social Work—cannot itself be credited with the development of these techniques. It borrowed them from the United States. The other schools that have come to be established in the course of the last twenty-five years have not made any appreciable progress in this direction. (It may in fairness be said that this fact has for long been recognized and that for some time efforts are being made to rectify the situation.) Borrowing in the field of science is a legitimate and desirable activity. In the physical sciences it must lead to a healthy interchange and continuity of tradition. In the social sciences—especially in applied social science—this borrowing needs to be carefully scrutinized. The failure to provide a local social context to the social sciences and techniques is one of the weak spots in their development in our country. History, economics and anthropology have made considerable progress at least in the accumulation of descriptive material. Sociology and psychology have yet a long way to go. Consequently, social work which depends greatly on these latter two for the development of its techniques has remained undernourished.

Whatever the difficulties in the local situation the acceptance of a scientific discipline in social work has two important implications which need to be understood. Through its knowledge of social dynamics and the dynamics of the human personality, science has contributed to our understanding of the causes of individual and social problems. This understanding has led to a hope and faith that these causes can be removed. At the same time, an understanding of what at least seem to be the real causes of our problems has led to an undermining of the traditional approach to their solution—an approach which may alleviate but does not cure.

Also, science has brought out the highly complex and delicate nature of human problems which need not only human sympathy, sensitivity and devotion, but also specific skills. The person who would practise social work has therefore to be trained. The growing specialization and the standard of education called for in this training have led to the crystallization of a new profession.

The role of science in drawing attention to causes was not wholly new or out of harmony. It did conflict with the traditional expressions of charity and philanthropy, but the conflict could be resolved. New forms and patterns of philanthropic action could be worked out. Beginnings had already been made under the auspices of the Servants of India Society.

But the marriage of social work to professionalism was not likely to be easily accepted. Social work has all along been closely associated with the idea of personal sacrifice on the part of the worker—sacrifice of time, money and energy on the part of those who support or participate in its activities. The incentives for undertaking such activity may be provided by considerations which are religious, humanitarian, those of social recognition, or those of social advantages. To the extent that social work becomes a profession it pleads that even social work can be a way of earning one's livelihood. It also emphasizes that a readiness to sacrifice is in itself not a sufficient qualification for a social worker. It further says that in many situations a professional worker who has had the necessary training in skills and who, since his livelihood is provided for, gives his whole time to his work is the best fitted for his work.

Professionalism, however, runs counter to the basic premise of sacrifice and has met with opposition even in Western countries where by now it has established itself relatively firmly. It is therefore not surprising that in India this new approach should be seriously questioned. The conflict that results needs to be clearly understood.

There are a number of ways in which this conflict could be characterized. It would probably be advantageous to analyze the mental pictures formed by the professionals and the volunteers about each other. According to the voluntary worker, the professional is inspired mainly by monetary considerations, lacks moral or social ardour, is prone to mimic the West, is probably well-read, but not necessarily a good worker. He does not evince the qualities of pity, sympathy, kindness, etc. To the professional, the voluntary leader appears to be a narrow-mined, intolerant busybody who is guided probably by good intentions and kindness, but has no understanding of social problems. He is inclined to be ambitious and is in most cases striving for social recognition. If he is a constructive worker then he is in addition a righteous individual who tends to seek authority in the words of Gandhi and feels insecure and is intolerant whenever this authority is questioned.

As in the case of all groups which view each other with apprehension, these mental pictures, true in part, are largely vitiated by prejudices and misunderstanding. Beyond them, however, is an even greater reality, viz., that the professional as well as the voluntary social worker have something specific to contribute to social work. If the professional can bring training and the skill of a specialist, without which the intricate problems of a modern society cannot be tackled, the volunteer brings to social work the interest and confidence of the community. And if the cause of social work is not to go by default, immediate and concerted action is required on the part of both.

The historical background and the analysis given above will have served their purpose if they can help us in arriving at a common outlook, a common philosophy, a common set of attitudes toward the problems of social work. Suggestions for such a framework are given below.

One of the very first questions that arise in the discussion of a philosophy of social work is that of motivation. It has been observed that the type of motivation that characterizes a social worker considerably influences his relationship with the persons or groups with whom he works. There is a variety of motivations—religious, humanitarian, economic, etc.—and it is doubtful how far a discussion of the desirability of one particular type over the others can really have any practical significance. What is sought to be attempted here therefore is not to enter into their relative merits but to present what appears to the writer to be a set of attitudes which are congruous with our past traditions—humanitarian and religious—and with the requirements of our present social ideals of democracy and justice.

In any group the set of attitudes which we characterize as the prevailing philosophy of social work will largely depend upon and be influenced by the currently accepted social philosophy. The motivations, the patterns of relationship between the social worker and his group, the immediate and distant objectives of the social work process are all closely related to the governing beliefs about the ideal patterns of social life, of governmental and interpersonal relationships. In a feudal society normal social intercourse was characterized by the lord-tenant or the superior-subordinate type of relationship. The social worker took on the attitudes of a paternalistic, kind giver and the suffering individual was the grateful receiver. A pattern of equality in which the dignity of every individual is recognized must take its place in a true democracy. The social worker cannot be a bountiful giver; he has to be a participant in a process which has for its objective the enabling of the individual to help himself.

This new pattern results from the acceptance of life as a co-operative undertaking in which the social worker like everyone else is doing his part to make life more worth living. This does not mean that the social worker looks upon his work from a purely functional standpoint and that the sentiments of sympathy and fellow-feeling do not enter into the picture. No social worker—voluntary or professional—can ever develop a sense of urgency about what he does unless he is sensitive to human suffering in whatever form it appears. But the acceptance of this outlook on life does imply that we have given up any idea of superiority—social or spiritual—to the individual or group with which we are dealing. There is no place then for a feeling of righteousness, or for a sense of sacrifice, or for any other manifestation of vanity.

This is important from another point of view. A social worker who becomes himself involved in the situation he is handling can cause considerable harm to himself as well as to others. This involvement can be emotional, in which case the worker loses his sense of objectivity, or it can be the subtle involvement of the ego, where the person derives satisfaction from the consciousness of the amount of sacrifice he is making and the good he is doing to someone else. Such an ego requires that the person who is being helped becomes dependent on the worker. This is bound to hurt the personalities of both. An attitude of detachment therefore becomes a necessary part of the philosophy of social work. This ideal of detachment has been emphasized by Swami Vivekananda, Gandhi, and practically all Indian social workers of eminence. What they had in mind, however, was the spiritual value of detachment. But even on the purely mental plane, detachment becomes a requisite of the personality of a social worker.

If now we accept democratic values as one part of our philosophy of social work, it is suggested that the other part is made up by the values of science. These express themselves first in an appreciation of knowledge and of a rational understanding of our problems, and, secondly, in the incorporating of planning as an important activity leading to the prevention and solution of our social problems. If the democratic values emphasized the dignity of the human individual and the relation of fundamental equality between the social worker and the people with whom he works, the scientific values make a plea for the study of causes underlying social problems and for a programme of removal of these causes rather than the treatment of superficial symptoms. And, the democratic as well as the scientific values both require that the person who would express them through his actions is activity detached.

Social Objectives

So much for the personal philosophy of a social worker. It is perhaps now proper to ask ourselves as to what can be the social objectives toward which social work strives. It will probably be in the discussion of these objectives that the specifically Indian character of our philosophy and approach will be brought out. It may be safe to say that very largely the social worker in the West has been concerned with the individual and his problems; he has tended to work within a social environment without necessarily questioning it; he has tried to fit the individual in a manner that he could derive the best within the limitations of that social structure or environment. The work of bringing about fundamental changes has been largely left to the social reformer and to the revolutionary. In India, the line between the reformer and the social worker has never been clearly drawn and sometimes even the revolutionary and the reformer have been fused into one personality. Raja Rammohun Roy, Vivekanand, Gokhale and Gandhi were at once reformers and social workers in addition to being leaders in other specific fields. They had sought to bring about fundamental changes in social institutions and social attitudes. To a degree it may be true to say that often in their vision the individual and his suffering were lost in the mass of humanity whose lot they sought to change. It is significant also that institutionalized social service catering to the needs of groups of individuals was for the first time introduced in recent history by Christian missionaries of the West. The tendency to focus on the problems of the group as against the problems of individuals is probably a general characteristic of the underdeveloped economies. The psychological and the domestic problems of individuals lose their significance when the vast majority is clamouring for the solution of its physical problems of food, shelter and clothing. The social worker's job in India primarily calls for the fostering of attitudes, institutions and processes in the community that would lead to greater production and a more equitable distribution of the means of life and subsistence.

In a sense the goals of such an activity are the same as in the West. They are on the one hand to create an environment in which the maximum possible opportunities are available for every individual for his mental, physical and spiritual growth, and on the other, to fit the individual in a manner that he can derive the most from his environment so that such growth is possible.

The emphasis on the group is natural. It is also justified. But when social work functions exclusively on the plane of the whole group to the neglect of the individual, it loses much of its revitalizing force. A certain amount of ruthlessness enters into the process. Faith in the capacity of human beings to change and choose their way gives place to an impatience with the inarticulate mass. This impatience is at the core of revolutionary violence.

The social worker who deals with groups, (but deals with them) through the individuals constituting these groups, can never function in an environment of sudden change or insecurity. A relative stability of the social structure, its acceptance by him—even if within limitations—and a sense of security are necessary for the practice of social work. Change has to be brought about since it is necessary. But then it will have to be a peaceful change if the fabric of life is not to be destroyed. A peaceful change normally also means a slow change. What happens when change is imminent?

A solution is probably offered by the Indian tradition—specially as developed under the leadership of Gandhi. Like the reformer the Gandhian worker accepts the need for fundamental changes, like the revolutionary he also sees the need for immediacy, but this way of bringing about the change is such that in this process the values of peace, love, faith in human nature are not lost. In fact, the process depends upon the realization of these values.

The above discussions may give the impression that a social worker in the West, because of his preoccupation with the problems of individuals, is unable to comprehend the problems of groups or communities. To the extent that there is a tendency in some circles to equate social work with case work, this observation may not be incorrect. But there is a growing realization of the need to understand the processes of community living and to utilize this understanding for the forging of new tools of work in tackling problems of entire communities. The recent development of community organizations is a step in that direction.

But a difference exists, at least, in the situation in America and that in the Far East. The people of America—and that includes the social workers—are normally confident of the basic soundness of their social structure. They are aware that they are enjoying the highest standard of living in the world and that they have a sense of freedom which they greatly cherish. They naturally believe that this prosperity is the result of their social, political and economic structure. This sense of stability provides the environment in which social work for the individual can function effectively.

On our side of the globe everything is questioned. The intelligentsia is impatient for change—fundamental changes in the social as well as the economic aspects of our life. The social worker finds that he is working in an atmosphere of great intellectual turmoil where he cannot expect to have a ready frame of reference. The picture of the national economy is not clearly defined even on the ideological plane. What kind of attitudes therefore can he foster in the individuals with whom he is working? Should he ask the members of his play group to learn to follow the leader, or, should he ask them to develop democratic attitudes and practices? Should he inculcate the ideals of an economy of national self-sufficiency, or international exchange? He has no ready frame of reference. He has to give his own answers.

Therefore, social work like everything else is at the crossroads. Can we have a philosophy in this context? If the values of democracy and science have been presented above as two of the cornerstones of this philosophy, it is because of a belief that there is a fair degree of verbal acceptance of these principles. It is to be noted, however, that the formula of adult franchise no longer guarantees the freedom that democracy promises, unless it is accompanied by a much greater equalization of opportunities than is realized, and that science no longer holds the same magic spell and is not expected to solve all our problems.

Here perhaps is a case for recognizing more basic values. What these will be is largely a matter of temperament and experience. Words like *love, truth, social justice* and *service* that we use to describe them are so overworked that they have lost their magic. Yet our eminent social workers, as social workers everywhere, have time and again found it necessary to fall back upon such basic experiences or faiths.

CHAPTER FIVE

THE PROFESSIONAL SOCIAL WORKER

An Exploratory Note

View of Man and Life

The professional social worker views man as a biological, social and psychic entity. He thinks that human behaviour can be adequately explained in terms of certain "needs"—natural or acquired—which originate in the somatic, social and psychic aspects of his personality. The professional social worker makes no assumptions about man's spiritual nature. This does not mean that he necessarily rejects all such assumptions, but it does mean that assumptions regarding man's spiritual being are not a part of the social worker's frame of reference.

It follows that the social worker does not look upon his work as a means to "salvation," either his own or that of others. He understands, of course, that his client (the person whom he serves) probably has certain spiritual beliefs. It is also likely that the social worker in his own individual life has certain beliefs and convictions in this sphere. However, as a social worker, he conceives of his role as being limited to the physical, social, and psychological levels of functioning.

From the point of view of the worker's own motivation, the professional social worker does not enter upon his work with the idea of accumulating spiritual merit. He takes it up because

---

This note was presented for the consideration of the Working Group on the respective approaches of "professional" and "constructive" social workers when the Group met in Bombay in June 1964.

he finds the work satisfying in itself—may be even egoistically satisfying in some cases—and additionally because this is often his source of livelihood. It may be asked whether such motivation is socially adequate. Will it motivate a sufficient number of individuals to take to this kind of work and will it motivate them sufficiently strongly to overcome many of the inevitable frustrations in their work?

The social worker looks upon life as a co-operative endeavour. He believes that man's goal in life is to seek fulfilment through the maximum development of one's potentialities. The social worker is one among other professionals who help man to achieve this goal. As a member of society, the social worker is both a giver and recipient of services. He works in many diverse situations. He works with individuals, groups as well as communities. He works with individuals who are poor and need material assistance, with those in mental anguish, with those who are ailing in hospitals, and with those who have difficulties in their relationships with others. The communities with which he works are equally varied in the problems that they face. What is the characteristic contribution that the social worker makes in these diverse situations?

The Role of the Social Worker

In the USA and other economically advanced countries the function of social work is seen to be the promotion of the "social functioning" of human beings—whether as individuals or groups or in a community—through the rallying of their own resources and a maximum utilization of available services in the community. Some writers have characterized social work as an institution which promotes the full and effective functioning of the other institutions of society. The emphasis is on the area of interpersonal or inter-group relationships and on how to make them individually satisfying, mutually beneficial and socially fruitful.

In this area professional social work has developed certain well-defined principles which flow from its basic liberal-democratic value framework and which guide its practice. An important principle in social work is the requirement that the worker "accept" the client as he is. Such acceptance does not imply "approval" of a client's actions. It implies the suspension of moral judgement on the part of the worker, a genuine concern for the well-being of the client, and a willingness to offer such professional assistance as he is capable of. This professional assistance may consist at times of material help in the form of money or goods, but in a more important way this assistance is directed to the client's ability to develop and utilize his own resources. The object of professional service is not only relief but rehabilitation. The change of emphasis is more in conformity with the concept of individual worth and the goal of promoting full growth of human potentialities. The successful practitioner of social work must enable his client to help himself—whether is an individual or a collectivity.

If such independence is to be achieved by the client the social worker's efforts at help must be based upon his assessment of the client's capacity to utilize assistance at a given point of time and they must always involve the closest participation of the client in the making of plans for his rehabilitation. The client has the right to determine for himself the goals he would like to pursue. The social worker helps in the process. The social worker must always remember, despite pressure to the contrary, that each person he helps is an individual, has his own problems which are in some ways different, and he needs to be helped to meet them in his own particular way.

In rendering his assistance the professional's only tool is his relationship with the client*—a relationship which must be characterized at once by objectivity and confidentiality on the one hand and sensitivity and warmth on the other. The particular skill of the social worker lies in his ability to use this relationship constructively.

---

* In certain special settings the social worker may also be able to use the authority of his office as, for example, in the case of probation workers.

Body of Knowledge

Conceived in this fashion the role of the social worker is mainly to set a "process" into motion—a process of interaction which takes place at the social and psychological levels. The fact that what the social worker aims at is a process of relationships and not the provision of a set of commodities or physical services makes a great deal of difference to what he studies. He tends to concentrate on the study of social and psychological phenomena, the uniformities that one notices in them, the sources of motivation, the manifest and the hidden meanings of behaviour at social and psychological levels, etc. His methodology relates to ways by which individuals and communities might be made self-reliant and capable of mobilizing their own internal resources.

The areas of knowledge covered in the curriculum of a school of social work in India can be broadly grouped as follows:

(i) Knowledge about human beings and about society, drawn primarily from psychology, sociology, social psychology, economics, and, to a lesser degree, political science.
(ii) Knowledge about methods or techniques of social work such as case work, group work, community organization, social administration, and, to a lesser degree, social action.
(iii) Knowledge about, and ancillary to, particular fields of social work, e.g., medical social work, care of the physically handicapped, tribal welfare, etc.

Skill in helping individuals to arrive at satisfactory and fruitful relationships may call for knowledge and "programme skills" outside the limited area of the behavioural sciences. In the case of the medical social worker, for example, it calls for knowledge of the functioning and pathology of the body and its consequences for the mind and attitudes of the patient and his family. The need for such knowledge of additional areas or fields is normally accepted in a limited way. The professional social worker is identified by his area of professional function and by his approach and methods.

As against this, the Gandhian social worker is identified by his personal attributes and once he is identified whatever he does is social work. He can work on problems of agriculture, khadi, rural industry, or problems of women and children. Attributes considered important are: non-possession, commitment to a life of poverty or simplicity, and a dedication to *work for others*. The knowledge and skills he requires are specific to the type of activity he undertakes.

The Ideal Society

1. There is no clearly articulated picture of a society toward which professional social workers could be said to be working. In fact, professionals have not commonly thought in societal terms. This does not mean they have confined themselves only to the particular problems of their "clients" and have no broad vision. It does mean, however, that they have not usually looked upon themselves as belonging to a movement which is dedicated to attaining particular societal goals: this is so despite the occasional lip sympathy that professionals might pay to the concept of "social action" and despite the leisurely, somewhat idealistic overtones of presidential addresses at national and international conferences.
2. There is, however, one value which is basic to the tradition of professional social work, viz., the value of democracy. Beginning with the principle of self-determination of the individual client, through the processes of working with groups and communities, professional social work has incorporated democratic concepts in its procedures and approach besides regarding it as a value to be cherished in the social order within which social work functions.

Another value cherished in the tradition of professional social work is the value of the essential equality of human beings and dignity of the individual.

Indian schools of social work lay adequate emphasis on both these values in their training programmes. These values are at the core of the liberal outlook which characterizes American as well as Indian political institutions. The Indian Constitution, however, looks beyond the broadly liberal ends and speaks specifically of a socialistic society and of the concept of social justice. The implications of these for social work have yet to be fully spelt out.

3. It would seem that professional social work as it has developed in the USA and in India cannot be practised, without basic contradiction, except in a liberal, democratic society. Equally, it should be obvious that no society has achieved a social order in which full freedom and equality, except in a political sense, have been achieved. And even in political sense it is doubtful whether equality is fully protected in the generally democratic states. Against this background, do social workers have a role to play in extending the frontiers of equality to larger sections of the population and in making the concept of equality multi-dimensional? If so, how can they do it? In doing so, would a professional worker be taking on the role of a missionary or even a revolutionary? Is the role of a professional consistent with that of a missionary or a reformer or a revolutionary?

The Self-image of a Professional Social Worker

It is difficult to write about what image a social worker carries about himself. There has probably been no research done in this area. It is possible that what is said in the next few paragraphs is only the present author's image of the social worker's image about himself. However, even at the risk of presenting a somewhat refracted image, it may be worthwhile to put down a few points for discussion. Hopefully, a truer image will emerge as a result of further discussions.

One outstanding characteristic of professional social work in India is its youthfulness in terms of the total period for which it has existed as a profession and also in terms of the age range of most of its practitioners. The professional is acutely conscious of this characteristic. This may make him feel proud or apologetic depending upon the particular circumstance in which he is reminded of it. On the whole, in a country where age is respected, the youthfulness of the profession may not be an asset to its practitioners. At various points a professional who otherwise considers himself competent may find himself passed over for others who are relatively less qualified but older persons.

This has often given the professional social worker a feeling that he has not yet been recognized by society. This lack of recognition may be experienced by the social worker in two ways. At a somewhat superficial level he may feel that he is not given the status which is worthy of his training and equipment. At another level he may have the feeling that he has not been given a chance to prove himself.

The professional social worker is also conscious of his being highly educated. He regards himself as being scientific in his approach. The word *scientific* is, however, used in a variety of ways. Sometimes it seems to suggest that the person who regards himself as scientific only means that he is not sentimental. He claims that his methods are based upon tested knowledge and that his work is oriented to the treatment of causes rather than manifest symptoms. Whether the professional social worker is truly as rational in his approach as he thinks is a moot point.

The professional social worker also regards himself as "progressive" or "liberal" in his outlook. He uses these words to contrast with what he considers to be the "traditional" and "outmoded" outlook that he attributes to the Gandhian social workers and the small-town, untrained, volunteer social workers. The professional social worker also likes to think of himself as being essentially democratic. This is a matter of value with him.

As He Appears to Others

To others who have been traditionally engaged in social work, the professional social worker negates all their normal associations with the term *social work*. He claims to have done no self-sacrifice in undertaking the work that he has chosen. He does not find it awkward to admit that he is earning his livelihood by the work that he does. Consequently, some persons would not regard the professional social worker as a social worker at all. They would regard him as an "officer", a "technician," or a "mercenary". There are some who regard the professional as being "theoretical" meaning impractical.

There are also people who use the words *scientific* and *training* as though they were a part of a mystique. They ask for "scientific training" without being aware of what exactly it involves and assume that every person who has undergone some kind of a training is likely to have the right answers to all the problems in the area of social work.

A Third Image

It is possible to give a third image of the social worker which is probably nearer the truth at least in the opinion of the present author.

1. Admittedly, the professional social worker has read and learnt much during his two-year period of training. The difficulty arises because he has not been able to perceive any meaningful relationship between his own experiences and much of what he has read. His knowledge, therefore, is not yet completely a part of his working apparatus despite the long hours he has spent in attending to his fieldwork. This difficulty arises partly because of the foreign textbooks which are used but also because of the lack of definition of the exact role he is going to play in the field for which he is being trained. With the exception of the fields of labour welfare and medical social work, the exact role of the professional social worker in the other fields is not known to the student or to

the teacher. It is therefore impossible to organize his learning experience in a way that would be meaningful.

2. The professional social worker uses a different idiom from the one which is current among the older generation of social workers. It is an idiom largely influenced by the American textbooks that he has read and is inevitably characteristic of his urban, middle-class upbringing. It is not only a question of using particular words which are part of the jargon of any new profession. It is rather a matter of the conflict of points of view. It may even be that the kinds of problems we identify as needing a social worker's attention are really not the problems which should claim priority in a country where a large section of the population is struggling for survival.

3. The professional social worker is secular in his outlook and generally democratic in his impulses. He looks upon his work as a job in which he is interested and which to him is worth doing. At best he has a certain commitment to the kind of work that he has chosen, but he would rarely call it his "mission". In recent years, the entire group of social workers along with the other men of the younger generation, has escaped the impact of any strong idealistic movement. Students who are now being admitted to the schools of social work were born after 1940 and have, as a rule, not experienced the excitement or the idealism of the generation which was born prior to independence. Professional education has also not given him the sense of serving a cause. Yet, all sections of opinion in our society seem to associate a certain sense of idealistic commitment with social workers, which they do not expect from members of other professions. It may therefore be useful to consider whether this feeling of belonging to a movement should form a part of the social worker's preparation.

CHAPTER SIX

THE PROFESSIONAL SOCIAL WORKER AND THE COMMUNITY

So far the term *social work* has not been clearly defined. Relatively, the term *social worker* is less ambiguous; and yet, even here, there are at least three or four different types of functionaries that are recalled to one's mind when the words *social worker* are used. There is the philanthropist who, either out of genuine social concern and perception of social needs or out of less socially-oriented motives, becomes the provider of funds by which social work activity becomes possible. He figures very prominently in the sphere of voluntary social work. He is often a person who has achieved success and leadership in the economic sphere. He does not concern himself with the day-to-day problems of organizing or administering a service, but in the background he is an important person. He is respected as a leader in society.

Then there is the social reformer, the leader of ideas. As a leader of ideas, he is both an iconoclast and a visionary, a critic of the old and a proponent of the new. Being a leader of ideas, he has his followers as well as his critics. His essential role is to get new ideas and new values accepted through precept and example.

Based on a talk given before the First Conference of Social Work in Colombo, Ceylon (1959).

Then there is the individual social worker who may be the head of an organization or a worker who fills smaller specific roles. He gives his time and his ability to the building of particular institutions. He often works free, and if not free, at a great sacrifice to himself. He is devoted to his work and is motivated by a spirit of service towards his fellowmen.

Somewhat different from all these three is the present-day professional social worker. He is also motivated by the spirit of service and of genuine interest in the work that he does, but unlike the others he usually makes his living by his work and has undergone a period of systematic preparation for the type of work that he does.

The term *social worker* may bring to one's mind any one of these different types of workers who contribute to the growth of social endeavour in the community. Each of these four types stands in a different relationship to the community and has a different type of contribution to make. In this chapter, we shall discuss the role of the professional social worker in the community.

Traditionally, a social worker was one who gave help to the needy. He did so out of a sense of calling. He was not required to do so and he responded spontaneously out of his own sense of social responsibility. He did not expect any reward. Most of the help that he gave was in the nature of immediate relief and physical care, but the kind of help given was not central to the calling of a social worker. He could be a layman or a doctor, a lawyer or any other professional; depending upon his own equipment, he would give one out of a variety of the types of help. But so long as he offered his help on his own, without expectation of reward and even at some sacrifice to himself, he was regarded as a social worker. In this sense, the community's concept of a social worker was not very different from its concept of a socially responsible citizen—a person who gave his time and resources for helping the community to meet some of its problems and who promoted the organization of help and services for its needy sections. In this sense, a social worker cannot be a professional, not only because he earns his living by his work, but also and primarily because social work, so conceived, is not a specialized activity. It does not require any special preparation.

If therefore we now speak of a professional social worker, we do so not only in the sense that the person so designated earns his living by doing what was traditionally regarded as social work but in the sense that he has an area of special contribution—a contribution which is different from that of other professionals and which he is able to make because of his special preparation for the task. This special contribution seems to lie in the area of interrelationships between individuals and between individuals and groups. It also lies in stimulating those processes in the community whereby a community begins to look upon itself as an entity and functions to meet its own problems and to plan for its own growth. The social worker makes this contribution in a variety of settings: he may function by himself or, as often happens, in co-operation with one or more of the other professions. The art of helping individuals and small groups without making them dependent or without depriving them of their self-respect came naturally to members of a small homogeneous community. In the growingly complex urban as well as rural communities, where relationships have tended to become more and more impersonal, the process of helping individuals and groups has tended to become formalized and institutionalized. The social worker emerges as a specialized functionary in this area.

What is the role of this new functionary—the professional social worker? What is his characteristic point of view? What is the nature of the contribution that he can make to community life? These questions have to be answered against the background of the kind of preparation that the social worker has had, of the sense of values that he has developed, and the position that the occupies in the community. The preparation of the social worker emphasizes the rational, scientific approach to social problems. He has been given an understanding of the various types of problems that beset a community, an insight into the processes that are operative within a community, an appreciation of why individuals behave in particular ways, the hopes and fears that they entertain, their various needs, and the ways in which these needs can be met. He has been taught that the norms by which individuals and groups live are related to the peculiar combination of geophysical, social, economic and historical circumstances that characterize them. He has learnt that individuals as well as societies can, and do, change.

This training and preparation has helped the professional social worker to develop certain definite values. As a social worker, he has developed respect for the individual personality and has come to examine all social measures in terms of their implication for the individual. As a scientist, he seeks to develop an attitude of objectivity which means not only that he is free from bias but also that he is uninvolved and aware in the broadest sense of the term. The great importance that the social worker attaches to self-awareness is also one aspect of this need for objectivity. Knowing that individuals change, the social worker must strive to keep himself free from the prejudice that individuals are innately good or bad. He must also accept the fundamental equality of all individuals as human beings. He cannot therefore be condescending or paternalistic in the services that he offers. He must do everything to foster the self-respect of the individual and the group that he helps. His success is to be judged by the extent to which he is able to help others to help themselves.

The social worker has to bring his scientific outlook and his particular sense of values to bear upon all the work that he undertakes. As a worker, he must begin by first knowing the community in which he functions. His special contribution in this direction is the discovery and the interpretation of social needs. There are problems that exist but are not perceived as such by the community. The needs of the villager who comes into the city and seeks to make adjustments to a new environment; the needs of the individual who finds himself torn between the claims of the joint family and his own immediate aspirations; the many ways in which the norms of the extended family find themselves at variance with the cultural complex generated by an industrialized and urbanized pattern of living—all these lead to the emergence of new problems. They have to be anticipated, understood and interpreted. The social worker with his specialized preparation in the social sciences is equipped to undertake this task for the benefit of the community. In fulfilling this obligation he has to utilize all available channels such as the newspaper, the radio, the legislature lobby, the forum of public organizations, and memberships of executive boards of agencies.

Just as a social worker can help in the discovery of needs, so must he help in the discovery of resources—organizational, personnel and monetary. He must study the known and potential leadership in the community and work with it in the mobilization of resources for meeting social needs. The volunteer and the lay-leader will always play an important role in the field of social welfare. This is so not only because our personnel resources will always continue to be short of our requirements, but because the voluntary worker has a distinctive contribution to make in the field of social welfare. He symbolizes the readiness and the spontaneity with which a democratic community will respond to its own internal problems. It is the function of the professional to seek the volunteer's interest and participation and to enable him to find opportunities for creative work.

The professional social worker can also make a contribution in the formulation of social policy. He must help in spelling out all the implications of a new service to its individual recipients and to the community as a whole. He has to help in outlining specific programmes in pursuance of a broad social policy and, further, in the execution of these policies and programmes in the field. The nature of the contribution that a social worker can make in the field depends upon the number of such workers available for employment. If the training of social workers is done only at the graduate level, and is restricted to small numbers, it is obvious that these workers will not be easily available for direct work with the recipients of a service. They could probably be employed only at the administrative and supervisory levels. This is specially so in the countries of our region where the percentage of graduates to the total population is very small and no service can be adequately manned with persons trained at this level.

The ability of the professional social worker to fulfil this broad role depends on the one hand upon the adequacy or otherwise of the preparation that he has undergone and, on the other, upon the position that he occupies in the community. The emergence of a new professional group is bound to raise some questions and doubts in the minds of those who have been working in that particular field prior to its becoming professionalized. A certain balance of relationships has to be arrived at between the new professionals and the earlier workers who had prepared themselves for the job primarily through apprenticeship. The situation in the field of social work is still marked by a state of relative uncertainty. The social worker has to gain acceptance not only from those who worked and still continue to work in paid positions without the benefit of prior training but also from those who are engaged in social work in a purely voluntary capacity. This situation has characterized nearly every community, but it has been further complicated in countries of our region by the fact that the training programmes are largely based on the models that had evolved in communities very different from our own. This has meant that the usual distance in knowledge, concepts and attitudes, which would ordinarily have existed between the professionals and the lay-members of the social work fraternity, is further increased by the cultural differential between the values of this training programme and the accepted values of the community. We find that the professional social worker begins to speak of the need for an emphasis upon rehabilitative programmes when the rest of the community is still busy finding the wherewithal for first-aid and relief measures. He emphasizes correction when the community is still struggling with its ideas of restraint and punishment. He emphasizes the emotional aspects of the needs and services when the community is aiming at minimum material benefits. He pleads for individuation in care when the community would be satisfied with the provision of some amenities on a mass and group level. This difference between the orientations of the professional social worker and the volunteer leader often lays the former open to the charge of being merely academical or theoretical.

There is also another aspect to this relationship between the professional social worker and the community. To the extent that the professional social worker is technically competent, he comes to assume a certain leadership in his field. There is often an ambiguity regarding the nature of this leadership and of the extent to which it may constitute a threat to the status of the lay leader. The professional has to realize that his contribution to the development of social welfare services has to be very different from that of the lay leader. There are two factors that characterize the position of the lay leader which, by the very nature of the situation, cannot characterize the professional. The lay leader is accepted by the rest of the community as being more identified with the community than the professional can be. The very fact of his being non-professional makes his point of view more meaningful to them. He functions at the level of the community and is not open to the charge of promoting "fancy" services as a hobby. Also because he is a volunteer his disinterestedness is taken for granted.

A professional, on the other hand, is not regarded as one of the community. In so for as he makes his living by his work, he has a material interest in it. Very often he is bound by ties of loyalty to a professional group whose interests are not always regarded as identical with those of the community. Wherever voluntary initiative and voluntary contributions are required, the lay leader has an indispensable role to play. However respected he may be, the professional cannot fulfil that role. The professional therefore cannot achieve leadership in the community in the sense in which the word is often used. In his particular field his role is that of an adviser, not a decision-maker. He has to function in a manner in which his leadership is given unobtrusively through his expert opinion.

Consideration of the relationship between the social worker and the community must inevitably raise a question that

I have so far left undiscussed. This is the question about the role of the social worker in the context of social change. Is he a person who stands for the status quo, or is he an instrument of change? In a sense this question is surprising. The profession of social work has developed largely in the context of social change. It was the problem of transition from the pre-industrial to the industrial economy that raised all the problems with which the social worker came to be concerned at the end of the nineteenth century. Why then should such a question arise? By his concern for the sufferings of those who were affected by the process of industrialization and urbanization, the social worker showed that he accepted the challenge of coming to terms with the phenomenon of change. He did not try to run away from change, nor did he attempt to stop it.

The question becomes meaningful when one notes the emphasis that social work has laid on the need for adjustment on the part of individuals to their social environment. The social worker was concerned with the individual and he was preoccupied in helping him to overcome his problems. Inevitably, he tended to trace these problems to the inadequacies in the individual. His efforts seemed to be orientated to helping the individual to accept the reality. He did not often raise questions about the justice or the fairness of the particular manner in which the reality factors arranged themselves. The protest against an existing social institution and against an outmoded set of values was often voiced and led by the social reformer. The professional social worker did not figure prominently in this field of endeavour. This gave rise to the suspicion that the social worker was unable to function in the context of and for the promotion of social change.

There is something in the very situation in which the social worker normally functions which strengthens this misconception about the social worker. The social worker tries to help individuals and groups on behalf of the larger community. In normal course, he takes the society and its set of values as given and expects the individuals or the groups to make the necessary adjustments. This should not, however, mean that he cannot at all raise any question regarding the values of his community. In fact, he has learnt from his social science that patterns of human behaviour and belief have a relative significance. They are subject to change and, with changes in the economic and technological environment, a change in the patterns of behaviour is nearly always necessary. As a scientist, he has to accept change, and as a worker he has to work for its promotion in the desired direction.

Yet, in working for this change, a social worker cannot utilize any and all means. A state of order is necessary if he has to function at all. The ways of violence and of coercion are not open to him. He cannot become a part, let alone be a spearhead, of a movement that calls for change in a way that it will very likely disrupt the very basis of orderly existence. He is not a "revolutionary" in this sense. He is at best a "reformer," and if he were ever to don the mantle of a revolutionary he could do so only as a *satyagrahi*. If he finds the values governing the institutionalized framework of society so unacceptable as to revolt his very conscience, the way open to him is to appeal to the conscience of society through his readiness to suffer for his convictions. But very few have the courage and the call for such supreme sacrifice. They are the path-finders of humanity and no profession may claim them for itself. The link between them and the social worker is the link of a concern for the underprivileged, the pariahs of society. This is a link that should bring together not only social workers but all citizens. That link is an index of our civilization.

Before we conclude, parts of an oath that some social work students and their teachers had administered to themselves may be given:

1. I shall serve to the best of my ability the depressed, the handicapped, and the needy.
2. I shall serve all equally and I shall try to develop such judgement, and affection, and patience that my service will heal ill feelings and distress.
3. I pledge myself to compassion, and words of kindness, and friendly sympathy that will enter into the joys and sorrows of all who are needy, or afflicted, or erring.

4. I shall never lose my faith in the value of every human being and the capacity of man to change his ways of life and thinking.
5. I pledge myself to work for loyalty within my professional group. I will work also for extension of such loyalty to all men and women who have the responsibility of serving my country and my people, in government or other official capacity.
6. I shall look not back but forward until the goal is reached.
7. Let me serve my follow men. That is all I ask.

These are worthy thoughts, and even if we cannot always live on the plane of nobility that they embody, the process of recalling them is an education in itself.

CHAPTER SEVEN

SOCIAL WORK EDUCATION IN INDIA

A profession is characterized by a specialized body of knowledge and skills, an area of operation, a code of ethics, and a certain degree of organization among the members of the profession. The professions of law, medicine and engineering are some of the more commonly known professions. Education as a profession has the specific function of imparting the necessary knowledge, skills and values to those who aspire to enter the profession. In the sphere of activity characterized by the older professions a person who has not undergone the specified programme of professional education is not allowed to function as a practitioner. In many cases there are legal provisions which prevent unqualified persons from practising in a particular profession. This is so in the case of the professions of law and medicine. In the case of some other professions the highly specialized nature of activities automatically prevents those who have not had the necessary professional education from practising in them. To the extent that the entry into a profession is restricted to appropriately qualified persons, the professional schools also perform the function of serving as a channel of recruitment to new entrants to the profession.

Professional education may thus subserve the twin functions of recruitment and socialization. The fulfilment of

---

Paper read at the Faculty of Social Work, M.S. University of Baroda, November 1962.

these two functions must naturally depend upon certain conditions. So far as the function of recruitment is concerned, its fulfilment must depend upon the extent to which, by legal statutes or by the high degree of specialized knowledge and practice in a particular field, the entry to a particular field of professional activity is restricted to those who have graduated from professional schools. It must also depend upon the extent to which the right type of young persons are motivated to enter the particular profession. This in its turn must depend upon the economic and social incentives that operate with respect to a particular profession in a given society.

Similarly, the fulfilment of the other function of socialization must also depend upon a variety of factors such as (1) the existence of a clearly identifiable and communicable body of professional knowledge and skills; (2) the availability of good educators; and (3) the closeness of contact between professional schools and the respective professions. These factors, in their turn, are governed by a variety of social conditions.

In this chapter an effort will be made to examine the social context in which social work and social work education function in India and to point to problems that seem endemic to the present situation.

Social work as a profession is of recent origin. Its professional character has not yet been fully accepted. This is so in nearly all countries and specially in India. There is a basic doubt in the minds of many as to whether there is a distinct body of theoretical concepts and knowledge which professional social work can claim as it own. There is a feeling that much of what goes into social work knowledge is really social science. The situation is further complicated by the fact that in India, as in other countries, people who traditionally entered upon social work activity were characterized more by the qualities of heart that they brought to their work than by any measure of intellectual discipline. Their orientation was more often religious than scientific.

There is also a third factor. Historically, social work was in the nature of a spontaneous response to a situation of need in the community. It was looked upon as labour of love undertaken voluntarily by the individual. There is therefore reluctance, if not opposition, to bringing social work activity within the sphere of a profession which after all is a full-time vocation by which individuals practising it normally earn their livelihood. In the sphere of social work more than in any other sphere of professional activity the lay volunteer and the professional come into direct contact. In India, social work has always been understood to be synonymous with voluntary service. The emergence of a profession and therefore of a group of persons who earn their living by their work was looked upon as an unorthodox, if not hostile, development.

The factors that have been mentioned in the previous paragraph are not new or unique to India. The difference lies in the fact that the profession of social work in India has developed at a time when the change from the familial to the contractual society has not progressed very far. Even the professionalization of the practice of law and medicine came rather early in our social context. This is still more true with regard to social work. This situation is sociologically significant, because it brings out some of the implications of a social change resulting from the process of cultural diffusion rather than through a process of endemic change. In the field of medicine one of the consequences that we saw was the simultaneous existence over a long period of time of the quack and the professional. In the practice of law, the opportunity for this happening was limited, because law had to be practised in a court of judicature and not with individual clients in one's office. Social work as a profession has grown considerably over the last twenty years. Yet, the fact that the concept of social work as a profession did not grow in India but came by a process of cultural borrowing has had its consequences in the manner of its development. There is a great gap between the ideas of the professional social worker and the ideas that inspire the traditional forms of social work endeavour. To a certain extent this gap has been sought to be bridged by the suggestive power of such words as *science* and *training*. The professional social worker is trained at the postgraduate level. The high educational level at which he is trained and the association of the concept of science and scientific training with his preparation have given him status. The lay social worker has, however, many unexpressed doubts about whether the professional is intrinsically a better or more competent worker.

This situation with regard to professional social work has also its implications for social work education. Professional education for social work in India may be said to have begun with the founding of the Sir Dorabji Tata Graduate School of Social Work in the year 1936 in Bombay. The House of Tatas, which is known for pioneering in new fields and also for its generosity, provided the funds for this initiative. It was indeed a difficult experiment. When the School began there were no known job opportunities for which the students were being trained. The School functioned, as it still does, as an independent institution outside the university. In a country where a university degree is greatly valued and is often a requirement for good jobs, this was indeed a bold step. During the years 1939–42 the School admitted a small number of students every alternate year. The faculty consisted of the Director who was an American and two Indian social scientists who had their training in the United States. They are joined by another Indian social scientist who had received his education in India.

These teachers decided to organize the training at the postgraduate level. In this decision an important factor must have been their concept of what the trainees would do after graduating from the School. It would appear that their intention was to prepare personnel to man administrative and supervisory posts. It is significant to note here that the diploma conferred by the School is a Diploma in Social Service Administration—not in Social Work.

The decision to organize the courses at the postgraduate level was bound to have one major consequence. The workers trained at this level could not become available to a large number of social work institutions whose resources were certainly less adequate than those of the government. The professional workers could expect to be employed only at the higher supervisory and administrative positions. These positions were available only in government and in industry.

There was, however, the difficulty of there being no defined posts of this category for which the students were being trained. Training of social workers at the post-graduate level was in this sense an act of faith. The staff of the School, especially its first and second Directors, had to perform the difficult task of attending to the training of their students, of simultaneously making the community aware of the new concept of social work, and of interpreting the role of the School in this field. They had gradually to develop work opportunities by discussions with the government administrators, industrialists and others who were in a position to create new posts requiring social work knowledge. One of the first such posts created was that of a welfare officer in an industrial establishment. Curiously enough, this was an entirely new job which had never been looked upon as being in the sphere of social work either in the United States or in the United Kingdom. The rationale for including this functionary within the area of social work was the fact that industrial labour was traditionally looked upon as an underprivileged group in Indian society and as a group for which special amenities and welfare services needed to be provided. The enlightened industrialist and the government offered these amenities and services. Even to this day, labour welfare happens to be the largest single area in which professional social workers have been employed. The social context has, however, changed considerably in recent years. The job of a labour welfare officer as defined by the government in recent legislation on the subject can hardly be identified as a social work job. At the same time, industrial labour is much better organized and better able to look after its own interests that it was twenty years ago. It is certainly less receptive today to the paternalistic overtures of the employer. The position of the labour welfare officer is therefore rather curious and not very enviable. And yet, this is nearly the only job for which training given by the schools of social work is statutorily recognized as a condition of recruitment.

The other opportunities that were developed lay in the area of juvenile delinquency and probation where social workers were employed by the government. Even in this field the inevitable problem arose. The social worker trained at the postgraduate level expected a scale of salaries which was not available to persons functioning as probation officers. The government could not have specified social work training as a minimum requirement for this post. The result was that the field is largely manned by persons with no social work training. The professional workers did not enter this field except as a matter of second or third choice.

The logic of organizing courses at the graduate level is obvious. If social work as a profession requires for its practice an acquaintance with the wide body of knowledge developed by the social sciences and also with the specific concepts of professional social work, the training could not be imparted at the undergraduate level where the student would be both young and relatively uninformed. At the same time, the decision to organize training at the postgraduate level inevitably meant the absence of any direct relationship between the level at which social work institutions could employ workers and the level at which they were being trained.

Despite this, nearly all the schools of social work that were subsequently opened (and there are about eighteen to twenty of them now) organized their courses at the postgraduate level. For eleven years during 1936–47 the Sir Dorabji Tata Graduate School of Social Work (now known as the Tata Institute of Social Sciences) was the only school in the country. In 1947–48 the second school was established in Delhi. This was the first school to be established as a part of a university. The fact that such a school could be established was itself a partial recognition of the academic status of social work education. The school was organized at the postgraduate level and prepared students for the Master of Arts Degree in Social Work. There were many persons who looked askance at the award of a master's degree for a professional subject in which there was no basic bachelor's degree.

Within less than two years a third school was established as a part of the University of Baroda. This time the school was not only a part of the university but also constituted an independent faculty. Since then, about eighteen schools at the postgraduate level have come into existence. Most of these new schools are a part of the respective local universities. While the number of schools has grown and the number of social work students has grown to at least ten or twelve times its original size, the basic question still remains: what are the students being trained for?

This does not mean that graduates of the schools of social work do not find employment. Actually, they are among those who have probably the highest percentage of employment in India. But this is due partly to the relatively small numbers in which they are trained and partly to their being found useful in positions which are not definitely within the area of social work. The positions of research officers and investigators are an instance in point.

This means that in the absence of clearly defined areas of work there is often no clear direction to the programme of training in the schools of social work. There are only two fields which are an exception and where social work education is preferred. These are labour welfare and medical social work. In these two fields the teachers know the exact nature of work that the student is likely to be called upon to do on graduation. Labour welfare offers the largest potential employment. Medical social work is relatively a small field. But in both these the training given by the schools of social work has come to be looked upon more or less as a requirement. This is not the case in the other fields of specialization offered by the schools of social work, as for example in the other fields offered by different schools such as juvenile delinquency and probation, correctional administration, public welfare administration, rural welfare, tribal welfare, family and child welfare, etc. In none of these fields is social work training a necessary or a sufficient requirement. Persons with social work training may, and often are, recruited to these posts, but many untrained graduates are also recruited to them.

One of the difficulties has been that persons trained at the graduate level are too well qualified for the low-paying field jobs and they are too young and inexperienced for senior administrative positions. The intermediary staff positions have arisen recently with the creation of social welfare departments in many of the state governments and the development of the programmes of the Central Social Welfare Board. But so far there has been no clear linking up of the personnel requirement of the many development services in India and the training programme in the field of social work.

It is obvious that in this context social work education cannot effectively function as a channel of recruitment to the profession.

The other function of professional education is socialization. This consists of imparting to the students a body of appropriate knowledge, skills and attitudes characteristic of the profession. This in its turn depends upon a clear definition of the role of the profession. The first problem in this area arises out of the absence of a clear definition of what constitutes social work activity. There is a confusion in the minds of most, not excluding professionals, as to the differential meanings of the terms social work, social welfare, social services, social education and community development. One often finds that these are used interchangeably and if distinctions are made at all they are often a part of the vocabulary of the particular individual. In India any thing that involves voluntary contribution, voluntary service, or even public participation tends to be regarded as social work. This confusion is greater because of the simultaneous development of a number of allied and yet unrelated activities. In India, we have seen the growth of the Community Development Movement. Undoubtedly, this movement includes some welfare programmes and services. But even more important is the fact that the whole approach and philosophy of the movement is one which has strong affinities with the social work method of community organization. Yet the relationship between social work and community development has been at best peripheral. In the meantime a new movement of Welfare Extension Projects—also for rural areas—has gained momentum under the Central Social Welfare Board. The points of contact between these two movements are only now being appreciated and the integration is yet to take place. One set of activities in the Community Development Programme are identified as social education. The same activities in the Welfare Extension Projects are regarded as social welfare.

Similarly, provision of good housing, building of roads, organizing schools, etc. are services which are not normally regarded as "welfare" services, but when they are undertaken on a special or priority basis for underprivileged communities by the Department of Backward Classes they come to be regarded, by association, as welfare activities. And any one who works in the field of social welfare tends to be regarded as a social worker.

One cannot deny that all these activities are legitimate and necessary, but they cannot be referred to as social welfare activities without causing some confusion in the minds of people. Another form of confusion arises from the tendency to regard every type of work done voluntarily as social work. Thus, a doctor or a lawyer who gives free services is deemed to be engaged in social work. Obviously, what he has been engaged in is his normal professional function and if this is regarded as social work it is only because he does not charge his fee.

These two or three sources of confusion are detrimental to the process of socialization in the social work profession. The concept of the professional function of social work has to be developed and interpreted to the community. It is only to the extent that such a clear concept is developed that the process of socialization in professional education can be facilitated. The beginnings of such a clarification are there to be developed. For example, in the first report of the Planning Commission, there is an implicit distinction made between the terms "social services" and "social welfare services". The term "social services" has been used to refer to the services organized by the government for the normal community such as the services of health and education. These services are social in so far as they are oriented to the individual citizen and are not merely services of the nature of environmental sanitation, road building, etc. Social welfare services differ from social services in so far as the former are oriented to the needs of underprivileged individuals, groups and communities within the larger national community. These services are intended to make up the leeway in a manner that the individual, group or community can begin to take advantage of the facilities available to the members of the larger community.

Social work has to be conceived of as a professional function. This function is exercised primarily in the area of the social welfare and consists of enabling individuals, groups and communities to rally their own resources in such a way that with the utilization of other assistance that is available they will become increasingly self-reliant and able to develop to their maximum potentialities. It should, however, be clear that not every one who works in the area of social welfare is necessarily a social worker, nor again is every field in which a social worker is employed the field of social welfare. Thus, in a primarily social welfare situation, there may be teachers, nurses and doctors whose skills are required in the same way as the social worker's skills may be required in a hospital setting, a school, and the community development agency, without any of these latter institutions being necessarily considered welfare institutions in the manner defined above. The speciality of the role of the social worker consists in the function that he performs as also in the methods he utilizes in the performance of this function.

If there is ambiguity regarding the distinct area of work covered by social work activities, there is also lack of clarity in the area of knowledge that constitutes the particular discipline. It is agreed on all hands that social work has drawn on the social sciences. Its content of knowledge has often been described as consisting of applied social sciences. In a way this is a relationship in which every profession stands with respect to the relevant basic sciences on which it draws. In social work the area of specialized knowledge which has been developed by social workers themselves is still somewhat limited. Knowledge in the professions usually grows in two directions—one of these consists of the body of general concepts characteristic of the particular profession. Usually the scope for development in this direction is limited and consists of a synthesis of concepts drawn from different basic sciences. The other direction of growth is the development of systematic empirical knowledge relating to typical problem situations and ways of handling them. Professional knowledge belongs largely to this latter category. This necessarily takes a long time for its development. In India not much work has been done in developing it so far and, unlike in professions based upon physical and biological sciences such as those of engineering, medicines, etc., the knowledge gained in other cultures and societies is probably not easily transferable in the case of social work. This constitutes another problem in professional education for social work.

It was pointed out earlier that one of the important factors on which the success of the process of socialization must depend is the availability of good educators. It is, of course, true that there are no absolute standards for whom we can consider "good" teachers. But, generally, it is agreed that in the field of professional education a person who would be a good teacher needs to have had previous professional experience. In India, the oldest professional school of social work has been in existence for only 26 years. Most of the other schools are less than ten-year old. Also, there are now as many as eighteen to twenty schools. One can easily see the difficulty of staffing these institutions with appropriately qualified and adequately experienced teachers. In this situation, the schools could insist on professional qualifications and thus choose teachers who had no previous experience of work in the profession, or select teachers who have had experience but no professional education. Actually, however, in hardly one of the schools do we find persons with previous work experience in the field serving as teachers. The solution usually found acceptable is that of employing young social work graduates or highly qualified social scientists who may have status in the academic world but have no work experience, nor a definite identification with professional values. This is partly a consequence of the lack of any vital contact between the tradition of social work in the country and the foundations of the professional movement in this field. Partly, of course, this is also a consequence of too rapid an expansion of professional education in the context of an urgent need for development

Another consequence of the lack of a vital link between social work tradition and social work education is the great difficulty that schools experience in finding satisfactory field work placements for the students. The teaching in the classroom is based upon principles which are valid, but are correlated to a stage of development characteristic of the country borrowed from. These are not often the principles which imbue social work practice in India, specially in the older institutions. The students therefore often find themselves exposed to the highly frustrating situation where classroom teaching sets standards or expectations which are hardly ever attained in practice in the institutions. This is a great obstacle in the process of socialization.

It is thus seen that there are obstacles in the way of social work education in India being able to fulfil its basic functions. An attempt has been made to show that these obstacles are not accidental, but are structurally related to the stage of development of the social work profession itself. In fact, it is only to the extent that they are seen to be so related that this analysis has any sociological relevance. It appears to the author that in its essential aspects the analysis is applicable to some of the other countries of the South and East Asian region where social work as a profession is a culturally borrowed institution.

CHAPTER EIGHT

PROFESSIONAL SOCIAL WORK EDUCATION AND TRAINING OF AUXILIARY WORKERS

This chapter is intended to provide a working basis for discussions on the subject of the "relationship between professional training and training of auxiliary workers in the field of social work". It raises questions and suggests some possible answers. From the point of view of the participants in the seminar the questions are more important than the answers. In the last analysis the answers are based on the experience of one individual. They are tentative, not conclusive. But, hopefully, they provide points of departure for the discussion to follow.

The task of the author has been made relatively easy by the working paper that had been prepared by the U.N. Staff for the Seminar on Social Work Education held in Munich last year. Working Paper 2, which was circulated preparatory to that seminar, has already raised many questions in respect of the training of auxiliaries. I have drawn on the points made in that paper.

Before one can go into the subject of the relationship between professional training and training for auxiliary workers, it is important to raise two preliminary questions: (i) Who is an auxiliary worker? (ii) Why do we need an auxiliary

---

Paper read at the United Nations Regional Seminar on Community Development and Social Work, Lahore, Pakistan, 1957.

worker? These questions are important because upon our answers to these must depend our view of the relationship between the two functionaries which in turn will define the relationship between their respective programmes of training. The working paper to which a reference has been made in the preceding paragraph has suggested some answers to both these questions. These answers need examination.

Who is an Auxiliary Worker?

Paragraph 36 page 19 of Working Paper 2 clarifies the use of the term *auxiliary worker* by quoting the following definition:

> A paid worker in a specialized technical field with less than full professional qualifications in that field who assists and is supervised by a professional worker ... . In some cases he may be fully qualified in one particular field and auxiliary in another field; for example, a teacher may be a nurse's aide on a part-time basis.

The two sentences in the above quotation bring to one's mind two very different images of an auxiliary worker. The first sentence speaks of a person with less than professional qualifications in his particular field. He is therefore a person who receives not only administrative but also technical supervision from a person to whom he is auxiliary. The second sentence speaks of one who is a fully qualified professional and is assisting another professional in a situation where the latter happens to have the major responsibility. So far as the particular job entrusted to him is concerned, presumably, the second type of auxiliary is more independent than the auxiliary visualized in the earlier situation. In this latter context it is open to question whether the use of the term *auxiliary* is appropriate. He is a fellow-professional.*

*The term *fellow-professional* is used in this chapter in reference to a person who has received full professional training in a field other than the one under reference but is working in a co-operative relationship with a social worker. It does not refer to other social workers.

The auxiliary worker therefore emerges as a person (i) who has training in skills for a specific job but is not equipped for wider or the more difficult professional responsibilities in his particular field, and (ii) who works under the supervision of a professional worker.

Why Do We Need an Auxiliary Worker?

The next question that arises in our discussion is why we need the services of such an auxiliary worker. There are probably several reasons that can be put forward for employing persons with less than professional qualifications in the field of social work, but they fall into two logical categories. The argument can either be that there are certain jobs in the field of social work which do not need professional training and can well be taken care of by individuals with less advanced training, or alternatively, the argument will be that while the jobs in themselves cannot be qualitatively separated, and while they probably need the attention of a professional, such qualified persons are not available. Our approach to the training of auxiliaries will be different in the two cases.

If the jobs to be done by the auxiliaries are such that they do not call for professional training, then, it will be wasteful to employ professional personnel on these jobs not only in the present stage of acute shortage of such persons but even later when, hopefully, we will be better off in this respect. The auxiliary worker is here looked upon as a necessary aide who will enable the professional to function more effectively by relieving him of the less specialized or less skilled functions and by letting him concentrate on his professional duties. It is of course possible that our evaluation of the jobs in terms of the kinds of skills that are required may itself undergo change with changes in our knowledge. But barring such a change in our basic estimate of the skill requirements of the job, it would appear that it would be appropriate to employ only auxiliaries in certain types of jobs. If this is our position, then, it is incumbent upon us to specify what the differentiated functions of the professional and the auxiliary are in different areas of social work activity.

On the other hand, the arguments for the employment of auxiliary personnel may be based upon (i) the immediate non-availability of qualified persons, or (ii) the paucity of resources with individual institutions which may not afford employing the available professionals. In either case it would imply that the employment of auxiliaries is here looked upon as a short-term and the second-best measure and is in the nature of a concession to the exigencies of a situation. If so, the programme of the training of auxiliaries in this case will be looked upon as a temporary measure to be abolished as soon as the country can afford to train and absorb appropriately qualified professionals in large numbers.

The situations in which the two different types of auxiliaries would be required are not necessarily mutually exclusive. It is possible that for our region there is a need for training auxiliaries who would do small specific jobs under direct professional supervision as also for training persons who would not be fully qualified and yet would be able to undertake some professional duties relatively independently. The seminar would, however, have to give thought to the question of the specific situations in which one or the other type of auxiliary would be useful. So far as the present author is concerned, he would be inclined to limit the use of the term *auxiliary* only to the first category of workers and look upon the second category as persons who are doing a professional job though they have not had the benefit of a full programme of training. The difference is important because in the latter case we will have to bear some special considerations in mind in the planning of the training programme.

It is here important to note one difficulty that arises in the definition of functions to be assigned to auxiliaries. There does not exist a clear definition of the functions and the status of a professional social worker at least in this region. Unless these functions are clearly stated and the jobs that should be entrusted only to professional workers are carefully listed, there will always be a difficulty in the allocation of functions and jobs to auxiliaries. Since persons with training and without training are non-discriminatively employed in similar positions, the professional often finds his status unprotected. He is therefore often on the defensive regarding any attempt to allocate functions to non-professionals if such functions can even remotely be shown to be related to the area of competence of a social worker. In the absence of a clear statement of what the role and the status of the professional social worker are, the latter is uncertain about whether he is not working against his own interest in making out areas where a less qualified person can be allowed to function. It is therefore of the highest importance to do such a listing of jobs for the professional so that the task of defining the jobs of auxiliaries can be undertaken with greater clarity. It may not necessarily be possible to arrive at a common list for all the countries of the region. It may be more appropriate to work out in consultation with the governments of each country separate lists of this nature. It is obvious that such a list will go on being modified from time to time. But, at any given time, it will serve as an indication that certain well-defined areas of work are sufficiently specialized to be limited to the appropriately qualified and recognized professional. The indication of a separation of functions as given in Working Paper 2 (Munich Session) is useful as a point of departure in broadly describing the different areas of competence of the professional and the auxiliary. But that beginning will have to be followed up, if our approach to the training of auxiliaries is to be more purposive.

Four Types of Job Situations

It will become apparent that in the above paragraphs four different types of job situations have been visualized:

(i) Jobs limited to professional social workers.

(ii) Jobs which should be filled by professionals but are temporarily filled by professionals as well as by less qualified persons.

(iii) Jobs for auxiliaries.

(iv) Jobs for fellow-professionals who may in special situations work as aides to social workers.

While the listing of these categories is relatively easy, the allocation of the various types of jobs to each of these categories is difficult. In India, labour welfare is a field restricted only to those who have graduated from recognized schools of social work. Medical social work and psychiatric social work (where it exists) is also largely limited to appropriately qualified professionals. But there are hardly any other jobs which have been so earmarked.

The area of aftercare and moral and social hygiene falls under the second category. It has been in principle recognized that the aftercare worker and the worker in the field of moral and social hygiene should preferably be a fully qualified person. In view of the immediate needs, however, special short-term programmes of training have been initiated as a temporary measure. The position regarding social education is not at all clear. The social work qualification is neither required nor considered adequate for the post of a social education organizer though, undoubtedly, the work done by the social education organizer is directly within the area of competence of a social worker. The short-term course for social education organizers is in some cases being actually organized in association with the schools of social work. The relation between the above two programmes of training, however, has not been clarified. The present writer would be inclined to classify social education as a field in which professional social workers should be employed but where persons who have undergone shorter periods of training may have to be appointed temporarily. This, however, is not the present position.

The training of auxiliaries in this latter sense is not anything new. In a sense it means the training of persons who will be able to do professional as well as less professional jobs in a short period of time at lesser expense and in larger numbers. The training of auxiliaries of this type has characterized the growth of nearly all the professions at least on the Indian subcontinent. In the medical profession we have had licentiates, in the engineering profession we have had diploma holders, and in teaching we have had special certificate holders. In these cases, however, the direct supervision of a fully qualified professional was not always insisted upon and the individual could exercise his professional skills independently within the limits set by law or rules governing employment. These training programmes were looked upon as temporary measures. In recent years they have been abolished and replaced with regular degree programmes. They were looked upon as programmes of a lesser quality of training and not as programmes equipping individuals for qualitatively different, limited jobs.

The task of distinguishing between jobs for auxiliaries and jobs for fellow-professionals who would work as aides is even more difficult because more and more jobs are becoming professionalized every day. It seems relatively safe to list the jobs of *gram sevaks* and *gram sevikas* (village level workers), craft and handiwork instructors, and *balvadi* workers (nursery school workers) as those of auxiliary workers. But how is one to classify the job of a health visitor, a nutritionist, a recreation worker, or a literacy teacher? While undoubtedly these persons do work in auxiliary positions, their functions have recently become more and more professional and their training programmes have been developed without a direct relationship to the area of social work. One may similarly consider the work of a diversional therapist, an occupational therapist, and a teacher of the physically handicapped. Are these jobs to be considered auxiliary to social work? Of course, a diversional therapist may often work as part of a social welfare department in a hospital which may be under the direction of a medical social worker. Similarly, a teacher who specializes in working with the blind or the deaf may work in a institution which is administered by a social worker. Yet social work education has had little to do with the training of these persons and a social worker has often little to contribute to the competence of these workers in their area of operation.

A suggestive chart is given herewith indicating the different areas of responsibility of the professional, the auxiliary, and the fellow professional aide in a few of the fields of social work in India. This is not a division as at present recognized. This is suggested as a basis for discussion (see Table 1).

Table 1

Field	*Professional Services*	*Auxiliary Services*	*Services of Fellow Professionals*
Social Education	1 Organization and administration of social education centres	1 Literacy programmes 2 Reading room and library	1 Do 2 Do 3 Do
	2 Preparing and working with the community and the neighbourhood to organize the programme of social education and social development	3 Recreational programme 4 Cultural programme 5 Information centre 6 Audio-visual education	
	3 Supervision and administration of the programmes of social education		
	4 Organization of training in youth leadership		
	5 Organization of training of village leader (Janta Colleges)		

Cont'd...

Cont'd...

Medical Social Work	1 To help the hospitalized patients to make adjustment to the hospital set-up by providing group-living experience; opportunities to express negative feelings and conflicts in play activities (in the case of children); programmes and activities to make hospital atmosphere cheerful; decision regarding the type of activities and programmes, the time limit (in consultation with physician); formation of groups will be the responsibility of the Medical Social Worker 2 To secure suitable assistance and services from other agencies in the community in helping the patient solve his problems, by referring to such agencies and interpreting to the agencies the patient's need for the same	1 Conducting the recreational, and cultural activities as decided and planned by the Medical Social Worker 2 (After the Medical Social Worker's decision regarding the assistance necessary to meet the needs of the patient, and the agency that offers such services) The auxiliary worker can follow up these by visiting the agency concerned personally, or by other means, and visiting the family members concerned, etc. till the actual assistance and services are better available to the patient.	1 In a children's hospital there may be teachers on the staff to provide educational facilities for children hospitalized for a long period; the teachers, though belonging to a different profession may help the social worker in his work by helping the child to learn and acquire certain skills which may facilitate the rehabilitation plan of the patient 2 Occupational therapy

Cont'd...

Cont'd...

Field	*Professional Services*	*Auxiliary Services*	*Services of Fellow Professionals*
Institu-tional and After-care Services	1 Planning the total programme of services, the daily routine with reference to its impact on the group-life in the institution as also on the individual (this will naturally include the whole area of grouping of residents, placing an inmate in a particular group, making necessary adjustments in grouping depending on situations as they come up) 2 Placement of an inmate in an institution (e.g. the Probation Officer's job) 3 Intake 4 Supervision of house-parents 5 In-service training of staff	1 House-parent's duties—planning and executing group living in a dormitory 2 Recreational and cultural activities within the structure of group life framed by the professional worker 3 Handling day-to-day problems of individuals in the group, also with the group 4 Promotion of hobbies, special interest groups, etc. 5 Getting preliminary data about the nature of the problem of an inmate for the purpose of referral to the professional worker	1 Nutrition 2 Nursing 3 Education 4 Recreation

Cont'd...

Cont'd...

	6 Interpretation of agency services to the board and the public (not exclusively professional area) 7 Therapy of individual inmates having serious problems 8 Handling of different group situations	6 Beautifying the institution—interior decoration, etc. 7 Playing the supportive role with individuals receiving treatment	

Relationship between Professional and Auxiliary Training Programmes

If it is agreed that the employment of an auxiliary worker is both necessary and desirable—necessary because of the shortage of professional personnel and the need to keep pace with the region's developmental problems, and desirable because it will help the professional to concentrate on duties which require his specialized skill—then the relationship between professional training and auxiliary training will have to be a positive one so that the former does not merely suffer the latter but systematically promotes and assists its organization. In the long run this is much more likely to protect and foster professional standards than an attitude of indifference, disdain, or even unreasoned fear. It is important that professional schools be "in" on this programme of auxiliary training and help in clear enunciation of its guiding principles and policies.

The training of persons who will be doing professional jobs without undergoing full professional courses presents many questions. The most important of these is the one relating to the possible loss of professional standards. If such a loss of standards is not to take place, we may have to provide for a number of safeguards.

It need hardly be argued that if a person undergoing a shorter period of training is going to be entrusted with professional responsibility the programme of training must approximate as closely as possible to the training of the professional himself. Ways must be found out to accelerate the process of training without loss of content. This is difficult at the best. So far as the theoretical content is concerned, this can in some cases be achieved, though not satisfactorily, by increasing the number of lectures per day. But, the same procedure cannot be followed in the area of fieldwork where the person is helped to develop appropriate skills and attitudes. This process cannot the accelerated by merely asking the person to work for longer hours. Even if this were possible a certain minimum of time has to be allowed for the process of assimilation by which the theoretical content is absorbed and integrated with practice during a carefully supervised programme of fieldwork. For this reason it may generally become necessary to limit the content of theory as well as field work initially to specific problem areas. This basis, however, should not become so narrow that it disallows any possibility of growth on the job on the part of the individual concerned. In order to ensure that persons who undergo a short-term course may still be able to take responsibility and continue to grow in their jobs it is necessary:

(i) to ensure that candidates admitted to such courses of training have the same educational background as persons admitted to professional courses; and

(ii) that they have, preferably, prior experience of work in the field which would enable them to grasp the various principles involved quicker than would be possible for a fresh graduate.

In order to enable the person to keep on growing professionally while he is on a job, special opportunities would have to be provided to help him to return for brief programmes of orientation and advanced training. In fact, if short-term training is not to result in the creation of an inferior caste of social workers, it will be important to see that facilities are made available to such trainees to accumulate academic credits over a period of time, and attempt to complete a full programme of professional training in this manner. This would require a re-adjustment of our system of evaluating and marking students.

Such programmes of short-term training intended for persons who will fill professional jobs should extend over a minimum of twelve months and should provide for intensive fieldwork experience in addition to classroom instruction. It is preferable that these programmes of training be organized and administered directly by the professional schools. This will ensure the necessary integration and community of ideas between the professional group and the persons who will be doing professional jobs without comparable qualifications.

The training of auxiliaries of the third category mentioned above is of a different order. Here, the person is admittedly doing work under the direct supervision of a professional and is entrusted with such work as is considered to be not involving professional responsibilities. Moreover, this programme of training is not looked upon as a short-term measure but rather as a permanent one, based upon a clear distinction of functions between the professional and the auxiliary. The principles enunciated in Working Paper 2 give the necessary direction for programmes of this type. These principles provide for:

(i) an understanding of the agency where the auxiliary will work and the methods or the particular skills he will use;
(ii) a knowledge of other social resources in the community;
(iii) knowledge from allied fields which will help him to function effectively;
(iv) an understanding of people and their common needs;
(v) a historical perspective of social work;
(vi) practical work experience under supervision; and
(vii) continued opportunities for training.

The training programmes for auxiliaries can be of varying lengths but it is hardly likely that they will be shorter than a minimum of six months. The educational qualifications for admission will also have to be different but in no case lower than the High School Examination.

The role that schools of social work can play in the organization of these courses may not be as direct as in the case of persons who will do professional jobs. They will, however, have a responsibility for setting down the basic outline of the concepts that need to be communicated to persons undergoing short-term training. It will also be necessary to see that the staff of such short-term training programmes consists of trained social workers.

While opportunities for periodic reorientation may have to be provided in the case of auxiliary workers, it seems unlikely that through such programmes the auxiliary would be helped to attain professional status over a period of time.

The training of fellow professionals is by definition outside the limited scope of social work education. This training will have to be imparted at various levels and should be the responsibility of the relevant professional groups. At the same time, if these professionals are to work in the area of social work either as aides or colleagues, it would be important to introduce appropriate courses in their curriculum of training to enable them:

(i) to grasp principles of working with people; and

(ii) to develop an awareness of what the contribution of a social worker can be in the area in which the two professions would operate simultaneously. Where such orientation is not given as a part of their regular courses of study, it may be necessary to provide for it through courses organized specially to meet this need.

The schools of social work have a contribution to make in drafting the appropriate courses for orienting fellow professionals to the area of social work.

The relationship between professional and other programmes of training has thus to be a close and positive one though the nature of the contribution made by the former to the latter must vary in the case of each of the three programmes listed above. Professional schools must in fact go beyond these three types of programmes and assist and participate in the organization of in-service training programmes and programmes of volunteer training as well.

CHAPTER NINE

VILLAGE LEVEL WORKERS

The general theme of this chapter is the "Contribution of Social Work Education in the Preparation of Senior and Auxiliary Social Welfare Personnel". The premise on which such a discussion can take place is important and probably needs to be explicitly stated. This premise is that the areas of social work and social welfare are not exactly coterminous, and that the preparation of social welfare workers need not—and probably cannot—be the same as the preparation of social workers. Yet there is a common core to the activities of a social welfare worker and a social worker. Hence, there is the possibility that social work education has probably a contribution to make to the preparation of a social welfare worker. This elaboration of the theme is important in so far as it helps to clarify that social work educators are not know-alls who claim to have a contribution to make to all kinds of educational programmes, nor are they in an expansionist mood whereby they would desire to incorporate every allied field of activity into the realm of social work. The distinction between the two areas of social work and social welfare is unfortunately not clear. Much that is referred to as "social work" in one country would be included only in the broader term "social welfare work" in some other. It does not even seem possible that a clear-cut distinction between the two

---

Paper read at the Congress of Schools of Social Work, 9 Tokyo, Japan, 1958.

terms or areas of activity can be made at the present stage. Speaking with reference to India, at any rate, the present author feels that the situation is just too complex to allow of any clear-cut delimitation between the two terms. This is probably so in the other countries of the region as well.

On the other hand, if there is no understanding, however approximate or preliminary, of the relative equipment of a social worker and a social welfare worker, a discussion of the contribution of social work education to the preparation of social welfare workers would be well-nigh impossible.

This chapter discusses the question of what, if any, is the contribution that social work education can make to the training of village level workers. An attempt has been made at a later stage to show how the work of the village level worker differs from that of a social worker. The discussion is necessarily limited to the Indian context.

The term "village level worker", by itself, is descriptive more of the administrative level at which the worker functions than of the kind of work he does. Even in India there are other functionaries who work at the village level and represent various agencies of the government. Besides the village level worker (male) who works as a part of the Community Development Administration, there is also a woman village level worker who works with village women and children, whether she is employed by the Community Development Administration or by the Welfare Extension Projects. This chapter, however, concerns itself only with the "man" village level workers working as a part of the Community Development Administration. The term "village level worker" has been used specifically to refer to the functionary of the national extension and community development agency of the government who works at the village level. Some information about the administrative machinery which he represents and within which he functions is necessary for understanding the role allocated to him.

The Community Development Administration (now the Ministry of Community Development) was established in 1952.

It began by establishing a certain number of "pilot projects" in selected areas. Typically, these pilot projects consisted of three "blocks" (one block normally consisting of 100 villages and comprising an approximate population of 60,000). The projects were established to see what results could be achieved by an intensive effort at an all-round development of the village community spread over a period of three years. Special funds in addition to the normal funds for development were allocated. Special staff consisting of a Project Officer and specialized professional staff in agriculture, engineering, animal husbandry, village industry, co-operation, social education, etc. was posted at the project level. The area of the project was divided into blocks, and each block was divided into smaller units of approximately ten villages each. Each of these smaller units was the area of activity of the village level worker. The village level worker was thus the field agent of a nation-wide development agency. He was expected to function in a multi-purpose capacity helping the villager in all the various aspects of his day-to-day life and was guided in his work by the experts at the project level.

There have been some changes in the administrative structure from time to time. The project has been replaced by the block as the unit of development. The specialist staff now functions at the block level. There has been a good deal of revision of the content of work of some of the functionaries. But, broadly, the context within which the village level worker functions is the same.

It is important here to note the approach and the philosophy of the Community Development Movement. If it is different from the development efforts of any other government agency, it is so in its emphasis upon the community. The movement is aimed at developing the entire village community through a process in which the community itself is closely involved. The object is not merely to extend services to people, but rather to make the people ready to take over their management. Association of the villagers and of village institutions is sought not only in the form of advice but also in the form of their active participation in the execution of schemes.

Most of the services offered by the administration are to be availed of by the villagers on the basis of their willingness to share in the cost of instituting a service or a facility. The village community can have a road, a school building, a community centre, or other physical facilities only on the basis of participating in its construction either through manual labour or by cash contribution. This participation of the people is regarded as an expression of the people's desire to help themselves and also as a means of making the community aware of its own entity. It has time and again been emphasized that the success of the Community Development Movement is to be measured not only in terms of the physical targets attained but in terms of the degree of change that has been effected in people themselves, and also in terms of the extent to which the community has become self-reliant in meeting its problems. To make the rural community to help itself is the most important objective of the movement.

Another important facet of the Community Development Movement is its emphasis upon the building up and utilization of democratic institutions. The goal is to see that at the village level as well as at the higher levels of administration the services are managed by representative bodies of the people themselves.

The village level worker who works with individual village communities has the opportunity and the challenge of translating this broad philosophy into practice. He has to perform his day-to-day tasks in such a way that he should be working closer to the objective of a self-reliant and democratic rural community. In a way every functionary of the Community Development Movement at whatever level he works has to be imbued with the same philosophy. But, with the exception of the Block Development Officer and to an extent the Social Education Organizer, none of the experts, administrators, or advisers have the same opportunity as a village level worker of meeting and working with the rural community as a whole. The Block Development Officer has to function as a co-ordinator of all the services and the village level worker as, very nearly, the conveyor of these services.

What then should be the equipment of such a worker? Before attempting to answer this question, it would be fruitful to examine in greater detail the actual work that he does from day to day. Recently, the office of the Committee on Plan Projects had made a study of the work of the village level worker. It was found that the scope of duties allotted to the village level worker included sixty-four different jobs. About nineteen of these jobs were in the field of agriculture, six in animal husbandry, one in dairy farming, two in poultry farming, two in fisheries, six in public health, six relating to constructional works (such as roads, buildings, etc.), six in social education, two in general publicity, four relating to office work and record maintenance, and another ten of a miscellaneous nature.

It will be seen from the above that the village level worker is a generalist, not a specialist. He could not possibly know all about each of the areas of knowledge mentioned here, but he has to know at least as much as a good farmer would himself know if he were literate and if he had access to books and literature on subjects that interest him. The village level worker is visualized as a person who would be easily available on hand to every farmer and who would know enough to give useful advice on the problems that arise from time to time in the course of work. There are other areas in which he knows enough to know when competent advice is necessary and where he can get it. Where he cannot give advice himself, he is the channel through which the knowledge of experts at the block level is supposed to flow to the villagers. But whether it is agriculture, in which he is more equipped, or public health, in which he admittedly knows less, his knowledge is never on the professional level. He is a high-school graduate who has undergone an eighteen-month training programme covering a multiplicity of subjects. He is therefore primarily a first-aid man, an auxiliary worker—an auxiliary to all the professional personnel at the block level.

But the village level worker is not conceived only as an auxiliary worker. He is also—even primarily—a community worker. He is the functionary who is expected to be a conscious instrument of change in the rural community. He has not only to know better methods of agriculture, better sanitary practices, better ways of caring for animals, etc., he has also to know how to motivate people to give up older practices and accept new ones. He has not only to bring technical knowledge to the doors of villagers, but also to know how the community can be rallied to use this knowledge. He is therefore concerned with the motivational processes of individuals, processes of unity and divergence that operate in a community, groups and factions, and with the crucial role of rural leaders. He is concerned even with the building of new leadership through promotion of youth activities, 4-H clubs, etc.

The skills of a community worker have to characterize all his other activities. The substantive technical services that he gives in the various fields in which he operates have to be given in such a way that the larger objective of an active, socially conscious, self-reliant community is brought nearer and nearer. The help that he gives should enable the villagers—individually and as a community—to be independent.

This approach of the village level worker is akin to that of a social worker. Without claiming an exclusive copyright for this approach and, even less, for the knowledge on which this approach is based, the social work educators can still claim to be in some ways specially equipped to bring to the village level workers the information, the skills, and the attitudes that should characterize this approach. This is an approach that characterizes the social work profession as a whole. Whether he works with individuals, groups or communities, the social worker is concerned not merely with supplying material services but also with building up the internal resources of individuals and groups with whom he works. This therefore is an area where social workers and social work educators can contribute.

There is also an area of substantive work that the village level worker does where social work educators can contribute. This area has been referred to by the term *social education*. The following are some of the activities included in social education:

1. Creation of an atmosphere for greater support and co-operation in the community.
2. Distribution and display of posters, films, pamphlets, books, leaflets, etc.
3. Organizing *Kisan Melas* and exhibitions.
4. Organizing campaigns for literacy, sanitation, etc.
5. Organizing youth clubs.
6. Setting up children parks.
7. Organizing community centres.

The above is not an exhaustive list of the functions of a village level worker in the field of social education. But it is sufficiently comprehensive to be representative. Of the above list, functions 2, 3 and 4 are obviously ones where the social work educator has no specialized contribution to make. On the other hand, functions 1, 5, 6 and 7 are the ones where social work educators can claim to be in a position to make a special contribution.

It is against this background that one has to consider the specific content of the knowledge and skills that social work education can bring to the preparation of the village level worker. In doing this it should be realized that the village level worker is not a social worker. Among his functions, the major ones require him to have knowledge and techniques which cannot be contributed by social work educators. He has, however, some functions which overlap with those of a social worker. And, what is more, his overall approach has to be one which closely approximates to that of a social worker. This is, in fact, an approach that must characterize all development workers at whatever level they function. Social work educators can only say that, after borrowing from different sciences and building upon experience, they have helped to systematize a small body of knowledge and skills which they consider to be relevant to these workers.

For a statement of the specific content one may begin with the list of "minimum social work content" for the training of development workers prepared by the UN Regional Seminar on

Community Development and Social Work, Lahore, Pakistan, 1957, which met under UN auspices in December, 1957. This list is as follows:

(i) Knowledge of the effect of deprivation—whether physical or emotional—on the attitudes and behaviour of people.

(ii) Knowledge of the importance of emotions as factors determining behaviour and thought. Knowledge of the fact that man is not entirely a rational being. Hence, awareness that change in the patterns of thought and behaviour is not likely to be brought about merely by telling people their faults or their duty.

(iii) Knowledge that behaviour is motivated and designed to meet some needs and hence the importance of understanding what a person is trying to achieve or escape by what he does. This can provide clues to the resistance to change.

(iv) Knowledge that the worker's attitude to people with whom he works has an effect on their response to his helping efforts. Hence the necessity for self-awareness and self-discipline on the part of the individual to make his own decision, etc.

(v) Knowledge of, and skills in, the components of the helping process and the principles underlying social work such as the right of the individual to make his own decisions, etc.

(vi) Knowledge of, and skill in, team work.

The process of helping the worker to develop appropriate attitudes and to use his knowledge in practice can be facilitated by (i) the use of the concrete instance in the classroom, and (ii) the use of fieldwork as a tool of education—not just practice. The organization of proper fieldwork calls for supervisors and fieldwork instructors. The worker should acquire enough knowledge so as to be able to recognize serious problems in human interrelationships when he sees them and to ask for specialized assistance when necessary.

The above is a succinct statement of what the minimum common content of social work needs to be in the case of all development workers. To this, however, must be added some special portions relevant to the training of individual functionaries. In the case of the village level worker, as conceived in India, it would be important to add the following content:

(i) Knowledge of the structure and composition of small groups; the formation of sub-groups; relations between a group and sub-groups.
(ii) Knowledge of the role of leadership; types of leadership; quality of leadership consistent with democratic goals.
(iii) Knowledge of the rural community; its structure and composition; the existence of different interest groups; the differential impact of developmental programmes on these groups.
(iv) Skill of working with groups of different age, sex, and stratum categories.
(v) Skill in promoting use of leisure for positive community goals and mobilizing the community for developmental efforts.
(vi) Skill in working with local civic institutions so as to strengthen them for accepting greater organizational responsibilities.

It must again be made clear that the content of knowledge mentioned above is not exclusive to social work. It has been drawn from sociology, social psychology, and allied disciplines. But social work as a discipline has sought to integrate knowledge from these diverse fields into one body for purposes of understanding and practice.

A point that has been made above as a part of the Lahore statement, and one that deserves special emphasis, is the use of supervised fieldwork as a part of the educational process. This is an area where social work educators can make a very effective contribution. In the absence of supervised fieldwork in working with individuals and groups, the training programme must remain fruitless in terms of its objectives. Social work educators are probably the only group which has a long and validated experience in this area.

In answering the question as to what contribution social work education can make to the preparation of village level workers, the author has so far proceeded in a purely analytical manner. He has outlined the job of the village level worker as he sees it and then proceeded to indicate what part of this job lies within the field of social work and for what part of it the social work educators are equipped to prepare him. The question whether social work education can help achieve what needs to be achieved within the limits set by the period of training and the previous educational background of the trainee, has not so far been raised. That question, however, is important.

The total period of training of the village level worker is eighteen months. Of this period the first twelve months are spent in giving him the basic knowledge in agriculture, animal husbandry, etc. It is only the last six months that are given to their training in extension and social education. The question therefore is whether in a period of six months the trainees can possibly be given the kind of instruction and orientation in social work that has been outlined above. Without being dogmatic on the question, one cannot but feel that the period is too inadequate for his purpose—specially when it is noted that the average trainee is at best a high school graduate. It would seem that the training period for subjects other than agriculture, animal husbandry, etc. should by itself be at least one-and-a-half years. In this respect, it is worth considering seriously whether the programme of Rural Higher Education organized under the auspices of the Ministry of Education could not be consciously so oriented as to provide for the village level workers of the future. If this were done it would also open up a career for the village level worker himself. Today, the village level worker with his present education is not considered equipped for any of the higher jobs in the development organization. If he had education comparable to a college graduate he would be eligible for promotion and then he could look upon the job of a village level worker as the first step and not find himself at a dead end.

There is also the question of the exact relationship between graduate education for social work and the training of the village level worker. There are two points of contact that can be effected. One is for the graduate schools of social work to supply the personnel that can serve as social work instructors in the training programmes for village level workers. The other point of contact would be for the graduate schools to accept graduate trainees with experience as students for their advanced courses. This latter would be possible only if the training programme of the village level worker is upgraded to be equivalent to college education, through the Institutes of Rural Higher Education.

CHAPTER TEN

SOCIAL WELFARE AND VOLUNTARY ACTION

The question of the role that voluntary agencies should play in the life of a nation has repeatedly been raised in recent years. It has become a subject of special importance since the end of the Second World War which marked an increase in the welfare activities undertaken by the state. In the United Kingdom specially, with the acceptance of the ideal of a welfare state and of the initiation of innumerable social services under state management for the various needy groups of the community, the question of the role, if any, of voluntary action became all important. It is significant that Lord Beveridge, who was the initiator of a large number of statutory social services under the Labour Government, should also have been the person who chose to assess and indicate the role that voluntary action could play in the life of a democratic nation. In England as well as in the rest of the advanced countries of the West, where democracy has had a long history, the problem of retaining the independence of voluntary action has occupied attention in all the discussions of this question. Sooner or later, this problem of defining the relative scope of the activities of statutory and voluntary agencies is bound to arise in every welfare state. To the extent that we have accepted the welfare state as our goal in this country a discussion of this aspect of the question is highly relevant. I suspect, however, that our own problem is somewhat different. Our problem in this country, and probably in all the countries of this region, is not so much a problem of retaining the independence of voluntary action as that of initiating, promoting and nurturing voluntary action. We have earned our freedom recently after a long period of foreign rule. The authoritarian forms of government associated with foreign rule are not conducive to the development of voluntary action which is at once the source of strength for, and an index of, healthy democratic community. This implies that, for us, a discussion of the role of voluntary action has a different and an additional significance as compared with the countries of the West.

For the purpose of this chapter, the terms *voluntary action* and *voluntary service agencies* are used in the sense indicated by Lord Beveridge in his report on voluntary action. He describes voluntary action as that action which is not directed or controlled by the state. He calls it a private enterprise for social progress. It is necessary for the sake of clarity to be aware that we are not here concerned with the distinction between voluntary as against paid services but rather with the distinction between the voluntary and statutory services. From this point of view a voluntary organization or agency is one which is initiated and governed by its own members without external control. It is possible that a statutory agency is relatively free in tis policy making and working, despite the fact that it is entirely financed by the state. From our point of view, however, its freedom from control in its working will not entitle it to be called a voluntary agency. Voluntary action presupposes the perception of need by the community or a section of the community, its assessment that the need can be met, and, its readiness to regard it a duty to mobilize itself to meet the need. It is an indication therefore of its continuing awareness of the changing needs of the community and the desire to retain the principle of creativity in social life. For the healthy functioning of democracy, voluntary action of this nature is of the highest significance. It serves as a training ground for the potential leadership of the community and helps to continually broaden the concept of social justice. Pioneering has been the major function of voluntary agencies. Their founders who have always been among the minority have perceived new ills and have stayed to persuade the majority to provide for their removal. The initiative and the sensitivity to social suffering, which are necessary for voluntary action, would be hard to find in a totalitarian state. Voluntary action also helps in continually focussing the attention of the members of a community on its problems and needs. It promotes the acceptance by individual citizens of their social and civic responsibilities and it gives them an opportunity to learn to work co-operatively. But more important than all this is the fact that voluntary action keeps alive the spirit of voluntariness of working without being compelled or required. A democratic way of life is not ensured by merely providing a democratic political structure. It lives in a multiplicity of small groups thinking and intelligently co-operating in the solution of a community's problems. This can happen only by fostering a spirit of voluntariness among the members of a community.

After this consideration of the general social significance of voluntary action for a democratic community, we may consider its specific advantages and disadvantages.

As indicated above, pioneering has been a major function of voluntary agencies. It is one of the points of strength of voluntary action that it allows experimentation. One aspect of this strength is the freedom of voluntary action to initiate work in controversial areas. A small group of people convinced about the need for a particular activity can come together and initiate work even if the rest of the community is indifferent, apathetic or hostile. This freedom to pioneer and to experiment is probably the first and the most important aspect of the strength of voluntary action. In our own country we have repeatedly seen that it is voluntary agencies that have sponsored lost causes and persisted in their endeavour until statutory organizations were established to undertake the particular services. The work of Thakkar Bapa for the welfare of the Adivasis and the work of Maharshi Karve for the cause of women's education are only examples of the manner in which persistent work by individuals against all odds has led to a change of attitude in large groups and communities.

Another important aspect of voluntary action is the relative degree to which it can remain independent of particular political trends. The agencies of government are likely to receive sudden support or to lapse into inactivity, depending upon the shifts in the parties of power.

Voluntary action is also found to be more flexible and free from bureaucratic rigidity. The officers of voluntary agencies do not have to work in an atmosphere where people are afraid of showing initiative for fear of breaking the letter of the law. Large bureaucracies tend to frame regulations which are more designed to keep people from doing wrong than to help them to do the right; a tradition develops by which individuals tend to do the minimum for fear that their actions might transgress the scope of work to which they are limited. Voluntary action has also the advantage of ensuring public co-operation. Voluntary agencies are born because of the general acceptance of a particular need; hence, the requisite atmosphere for the eliciting of general co-operation. Governmental agencies which come into existence as a result of statutory provisions may often fail in winning this co-operation, because of the lack of awareness and appreciation of the urgency on the part of the community as a whole.

Voluntary agencies have also the advantage that because of the greater proportion of services that are rendered by volunteers their operational costs are kept at a minimum. This last is an advantage that is likely to be abused. It might lead people to expect that voluntary agencies should do without any paid or professional personnel altogether. There is a need in this area for a clearer understanding of the respective contributions of volunteers and salaried workers.

Voluntary action is born of the desire of a group—large or small—to help meet an urgent need. This action may be in the nature of self-help or the help given by relatively well-placed individuals to those who are deprived. In either case there is no compulsion. In its absence, the emergence of voluntary action in relation to a particular need will depend entirely upon whether the need is perceived, whether those who perceive it feel motivated to act in relation to it, and whether they have the necessary resources to act. Out of these very conditions are born some of the limitations of voluntary action.

Probably, the most common limitation arises out of the limited resources that voluntary agencies have at their disposal. It is often found that this compels the agencies to work on too small a scale. Very often the agencies that are established are not adequate to meet the needs of even the local area in that particular field. It would be worth considering whether and how far our voluntary agencies are in a position to meet the demands made upon them.

This smallness of scale is probably due also to another characteristic of voluntary action, namely, the fact that it is often born out of the appreciation of an immediate problem. The founders of such agencies are not often aware of similar problems being faced by other communities in different parts of the country. This largely accounts for the uncoordinated and somewhat sporadic character of voluntary action. Enough thought or planning has not gone into its organization. Very likely, if the founders of an agency stopped too long to think and plan, the agency would never be born.

This sporadic character of voluntary action often leads to its instability. Organizations are founded without a certainty or even a plan regarding where their resources are going to be drawn from; and even if the organization continues to exist, it functions ill-equipped, understaffed and inefficiently. It is necessary here to say that all voluntary agencies do not necessarily suffer from these ills. There are, indeed, national and international organizations whose offices are better staffed than probably those of some of the statutory organizations; but the observations made above probably hold true about a large number of voluntary agencies in our own country and other countries in Asia. The total available resources within the country are so limited that even if all those who could, were to give, these resources would still be insufficient for the proper organization of our services.

In our own country this problem has become more accentuated since the last few years. The rich landlords are experiencing a sense of insecurity and want to hold on to what they have. The middle class, which is often the mainstay of such organizations by way of voluntary effort as well as for funds collected through small contributions, is finding it increasingly difficult to make both ends meet. The new aristocracy of finance and business is relatively free from the considerations born of religious and conventional obligations. They have yet to develop their own code of social responsibilities. In this period of transition, therefore, the normally poor voluntary agencies of our country are experiencing a special crisis. This seems to have at least two consequences: on the one hand, fewer new agencies are now coming into existence and, on the other, there is an increase in the number of existing agencies seeking "nationalization". This temporary crisis has strengthened the traditional mode of dependence upon governmental initiative, bred during two hundred years of foreign rule. The present, therefore, seems the most inopportune time for a consideration of the manner in which most voluntary agencies can help promote the welfare objectives visualized by our planners.

Yet, it is not certain whether governmental and statutory agencies can expect to meet all the welfare needs of the people. In our country where government has to face the basic challenge of having to raise the standard of living of the general populace, it seems unrealistic to expect that they will alone be able to initiate and organize welfare services, except the minimum essential ones. The danger of increasing governmental activity swallowing up areas of voluntary action is neither an immediate nor a real danger. It may therefore not be worthwhile to spend time on the otherwise vital issue of the independence of voluntary action. There is, however, a sense in which governmental policy will largely influence voluntary action in the sphere of social welfare. In this part of the world, governments have, of necessity, tended to become the largest single units in every country. If quick and even progress is to be achieved in matters relating to economic development, then, a certain degree of increase in the sphere of governmental activity in general is inevitable, given the conditions of capital formation that prevail in the underdeveloped areas. This has, however, created a peculiar situation for voluntary agencies. It has meant that they are increasingly compelled to look to the state for supporting voluntary effort.

The basic question of this policy is: in a situation where the government tends increasingly to become the main source of financial support, would it not be in the interests of efficiency for the government itself to take over these institutions? Our answer to this question must be based upon a consideration of the types of services and institutions involved. In the above paragraphs we have considered the strengths and the weaknesses of voluntary effort. In the consideration of this we have had occasion indirectly to notice the corresponding advantages and disadvantages of governmental action. It would be impossible to say at any time whether or not any particular sphere of welfare activity should be entirely left to voluntary effort or should be undertaken by the government. There can be no hard and fast rules on questions of this nature. There are, however, certain guiding principles that emerge both from a study of the historical trends in the growth and development of welfare services as also from an analysis of the advantages and disadvantages of the two types of services undertaken above. These principles have been succinctly stated by Henry Adolphus Mess* as follows:

1. Where large-scale provisions are generally recognized to be necessary and where it is of a kind which can be standardized without great difficulties and without hardships to government those provisions should be the responsibility of the state and it is probable that in most cases it should be directly administered by the state.
2. Where flexibility, experiment, supplementation, or exceptional degree of self-devotion are necessary, there is a strong case for the voluntary society though these need not preclude state co-operation.
3. Social work whose desirability is a matter of strong controversy must usually be left to voluntary agencies.
4. The promotion of mutual aid schemes requires both voluntary and state action.

* Henry Adolphus Mess, *Voluntary Social Services Since 1918*, Routledge, London, 1948.

It must be noted, however, that these principles have been evolved for a country where the state has had the resources to provide an increasing number of welfare services for its citizens. With us the possibility of the state being immediately to make large-scale provisions of welfare services does not exist. The problems that a governmental policy in relation to welfare agencies will have to face are of a different character. This policy will have to answer the following three questions:

1. How can governmental policy help existing agencies to function efficiently and grow in response to increasing and changing needs?
2. How can the government help promote the development of new voluntary agencies?
3. In what conditions and circumstances should the government decide to take over individual services and/or institutions?

There are two different ways in which the government could help existing agencies to continue to function effectively and grow in response to changing circumstances. One of these is by offering direct help in terms of finances and equipment. Our analysis has shown how, increasingly, the government will have to continue to undertake this function of offering large or small financial aid to voluntary agencies. There are, however, certain precautions that need to be taken if such aid is not to become wasteful. One of these is an assessment of the number of institutions working in a given field and the quality of work they are doing. Financial aid can become one of the means through which the government might be able to help develop standards of care and services provided by the different institutions. It is true that it would be impossible for the government or for any single agency to arbitrarily set down the standards that should obtain in welfare institutions. It would neither be proper nor fruitful. Primarily, this role of developing the standards of adequacy of services must be taken over by the agencies and institutions themselves through appropriate co-ordinating bodies in each of the several fields of service. Associations of professional social workers and schools of social work have a special responsibility in this sphere. The government can do a great deal in promoting the definitions of these standards by encouraging the existing co-ordinating organizations in the field of child welfare, adult education, youth welfare, and of social work generally, to undertake this task. But once these minimum standards are laid down, it would be expected from governmental departments giving financial aid that they insist on the observance of such agreed standards.

There are also other questions relating to the offer of financial aid in such a way that this becomes stimulative of further voluntary effort rather than becoming the cause of increased dependence on the part of the agencies supported. The details of the manner in which financial aid may effectively be given must be left for another occasion. Briefly, one might say that an adequate machinery for purposes of inspection and assessment, and also for the purposes of affording helpful supervision, is one of the minimum requirements of a programme of financial aid on the part of state agencies.

Another way in which the government might help existing agencies relates to the manner in which the latter may continually be associated with statutory action. There are two modes in which this association may be effected. One of these is to have representatives of well-established and recognized institutions as members of advisory groups helping the working of statutory services. It may be noted that this particular manner of association has been the practice of our administration from the days of British rule. The functions to be performed by the advisory group do not, however, seem to be clearly appreciated either by the departments or by the advisers themselves.

There is a tendency on both sides to regard nomination to advisory bodies as only a way of conferring distinction on individuals. It is necessary to see that such bodies are associated more closely and more regularly with the working of the services. This would imply convening meetings of advisory bodies much more often than is now common and, further, giving the recommendations of the advisers more authority in terms of their being binding on the executive.

The other mode in which voluntary agencies might be associated with statutory action is through the delegation of specific functions to such agencies. In the field of the care and correction of juvenile delinquents this mode of association seems to have been commonly accepted. We find voluntarily organized institutions being recognized and entrusted with functions of managing remand homes and certified schools; outside this field, however, this mode of association is hardly at all prevalent.

Another important way the government can help the voluntary agencies is through legislative action. Services in the field of moral and social hygiene, in the field of preventive health measures, and in the solution of the problems of vagrancy could be greatly improved and strengthened by appropriate legislative action which would help and support voluntary action. Here, at times, the controversiality of a particular service may be an obstacle in the way of governmental help, but there is a sufficient area of common agreement yet to be covered by legislative action.

The second question that is important in developing a governmental policy with regard to voluntary agencies is the manner in which the government might help promote the development of new agencies. To say that the government might initiate voluntary services is a contradiction in terms. Voluntary agencies, if they are worthy of the name, must be born of voluntary endeavour. It is, however, possible for the government to create conditions under which citizens will be encouraged to organize new voluntary agencies. To the extent that the government policy in relation to existing institutions is increasingly appreciated as one which is helpful in its supervision, guidance and aid, it will be found to promote not only the effective functioning of existing institutions but also the organization of new agencies.

The last question that needs to be answered in the formulating of a governmental policy is the one relating to conditions and circumstances under which the government might decide to take over, for management, individual services and/or institutions. Here, the principles suggested by Mess in the division of responsibilities between state and voluntary action should form one of the bases of consideration. It is clear that in the long run no voluntary agency can expect to institute services which will make large-scale provisions. It may often happen that voluntary action initiates services in order to focus the attention of the people on a particular problem. But to the extent that such a service comes to be considered as a minimum provision to be made for all people generally, there will be a case for the government taking over such services. Historically, services in the field of education and health have shown a trend in this direction. In European countries, unemployment insurance, old age benefits, and other measures of social security began as services offered by voluntary agencies to families in need. Their meagre resources, however, could never expect to meet the demands of the entire population. The state stepped in to take over the functions.

CHAPTER ELEVEN

A NATIONAL CONFERENCE OF SOCIAL WORK

In these pages, I propose to outline what, according to me, a National Conference on Social Work should aim to achieve. In doing so I shall also point out the conditions under which the conference may be able to achieve these objectives.

To begin with, a "conference" means a "conferring together of individuals". The verb *confer* refer not only to the act of meeting of individuals but also involves an exchange of ideas between them. A conference has therefore to be, first, a forum for ideas. The adjective *national* and the words of *social work* are indicative of the region and the subject matter to which the forum will be limited. A national conference of social work will therefore set for itself this very important objective of serving as the forum for the exchange of ideas in the field of social work for people of a particular national community. A question has often been raised as to how exactly we delimit the area of social work. With the development of the discipline and the profession of social work, the term "social work" has tended to be used to refer to the area of activity of this profession. The conferences of social work in different parts of the world, including the International Conference of Social Work, have used this term in a broader context to refer to the

Based on a talk given to the First Conference of Social Work, Colombo, Ceylon, 1959.

area of not only the social worker but also that of the health worker, the educationist, the lawyer, the jurist, etc. in so far as these latter involve or pertain to problems of individual adjustment and social organization. In some places this wider area has been referred to by the use of the term "social welfare" rather than "social work". It is obvious, of course, that a conference of social work is neither a medical conference nor an educational conference though doctors as well as educationists may be represented amongst its delegates. The doctors, teachers, lawyers and other professionals who come to conference of social work being their special backgrounds and equipment to bear upon the discussions of the outstanding social problems that take place at the conference. These problems and their solutions may even lie partly in the field of one or more of the specialities that they represent. Yet they do not look to a discussion of the technical problems faced by their respective professions at a conference of social work.

A national conference of social work is therefore a platform which is available for all welfare workers—social workers, lawyers, doctors, educators and non-professional lay leaders of the community—for the discussion of common problems in the area of social welfare. The exact definition given to this area naturally differs with time and place. Some problems which may seem of urgent significance in one country may be of no interest to welfare workers in another country; and even in the same country the significance attached to particular problems will vary from one period of history to another. As a forum for ideas, the conference must encourage all ideas—orthodox and unorthodox. It must also allow for a free play of the currents and cross-currents of thought in this particular field. No forum can be restrictive if it has to serve its purpose, certainly not in the context of a democratic structure of society. It has again and again been seen, specially in the field of social work, that ideas which have been considered newfangled and strange have actually turned out to be the forerunners of a completely new and effective way of approaching difficult social problems.

To fulfil its role as a forum for ideas, the national conference must be wide-based. This should be so not only in the sense that all the different professional groups should be represented in it but also in the sense that within the area of social work all the different fields should be represented in its membership. The needs of women and children, the aged, the handicapped, the backward, as also the welfare needs of the normal community must find a place in the sphere of interest of the conference. The conference should also be broad-based in that it should provide an opportunity for officials and non-officials, for government and voluntary groups to get together to do common thinking in a spirit of understanding and constructive criticism. It is only in this atmosphere that people will learn from their different efforts in meeting varied problems. They will learn from each of these points of view and also from the mistakes and pitfalls that have characterized their respective efforts. On the positive side this sharing together will generate a sense of community among all persons interested in the amelioration and eradication of social problems.

The stimulation and bringing together of ideas in the field of social work is, however, only one of the objectives of a national conference. It has another role to play in focussing these ideas on particular problems at particular times. It should help and develop public consciousness on new needs and problems that the community is experiencing at any given time. To the extent that the conference represents the consensus of all those who are interested in social welfare, its voice will be listened to by the community at large and by those who are in a position to make and influence policy. It is obvious that the varied membership of the conference will not always agree on every single issue. A body which serves as a forum for ideas does not easily lend itself to being used as an instrument of action. Even so, or probably because this is so, whenever there is an agreement on problems that need immediate attention, the conference will be able to add significantly to the effort to make them a part of the awareness of the people and to promote positive action toward its solution. The education of the community at large in the problems of social health is one of the crucial roles that a national conference will be called upon to fulfil. In this direction, the conference may use a variety of different methods and instrumentalities such as the holding of meetings, the preparation and submission of memoranda, the sending of delegations to wait upon policy makers, and the canvassing of support from individual legislators to promote and strengthen community action. This would also require the co-operation of the newspapers, the radio, the popular magazines, etc. In addition, the conference may find it necessary to have an organ of its own which will help the social workers to learn about developments in their field in different parts of the country, and which will serve as a continued link when the conference in not in session.

If, however, the conference is to perform successfully this role of an educator of public opinion, it must base its policy as well as strategy on an intelligent study of facts. A knowledge and a continual re-assessment of the needs of different groups and of the community as a whole in the field of social welfare, coupled with a knowledge and examination of the extent and adequacy of services provided within the community, is an absolute minimum for any organized action undertaken by the conference. Usually, this is one of the weakest departments of national conferences all over the world. There are difficulties of finance as well as of personnel in undertaking research and investigation which will enable the conference to fulfil this major role. There is also the difficulty of a lack of genuine appreciation of the need for facts. Appeals by social workers for action in particular fields are usually based upon sentiments. To the extent that this is so, it is impossible to establish any kind of priorities between the different needs. It should be the function of a conference of social work to enable objective studies to be undertaken which will help to establish the extent of needs as well as services that exist in different fields, so that at least an approach to the establishing of priorities can be made. A call for action based upon facts rather than sentiments will also merit the attention of all hard-pressed and hard-boiled administrators and public men. The fact-finding and research functions are also important in stimulating a process of self-assessment and examination which are necessary for ensuring continual growth and refinement in the pattern of service and the methods of social work adopted by different institutions and agencies. Social service institutions usually come into existence when problems have become too acute to be left unnoticed, and in an atmosphere of emergency. Once they have come into existence they tend to function by force of tradition. They are rarely characterized by later conscious efforts to re-examine the problem which they have set out to solve. Outmoded practice and theory are not very rare to come by in the field of social welfare. A conference of social work which represents the meeting of the minds of experienced persons should give a lead in emphasizing the need for introducing a rational element in the organizing of social services. The emphasis upon facts and research and upon evaluation is a beginning in this direction.

Another objective that a national conference can keep before itself is that of serving as a consultative and guiding agency for social service institutions working in the field. If it fulfils the role of collecting facts and of undertaking continual evaluation of the methods utilized by social workers all over the country, it will have to equip itself properly for functioning as an agency that can offer technical assistance. Every agency is not in a position to keep itself in touch with the newer methods and practices in social work that are being experimented with all the time. Also, not every agency can afford to employ highly trained professional staff. Even if individual agencies were able to employ such staff and to keep themselves in touch with newer developments in the field, they do not have the advantage of possessing a national perspective either of the needs or of the services required. The conference of social work has the potentiality of acquiring this perspective, the resources, and the expert personnel to offer a technical guidance service within the country. The need for such a service is probably all the greater in countries of our region where for years to come appropriately trained personnel will continue to be in short supply. A national conference is therefore called upon to undertake this service and to guide individual agencies at a higher level of efficiency.

The conference, however, cannot fulfil this function except to the extent that it is looked upon as a body which has the support of and which represents social work interest in the country as a whole. Guidance can never be forced. It can only be offered when sought, and the agencies will be willing to seek and accept this guidance more easily if they accept this organization as their own. The conference has therefore to earn for itself a place in the affection of social workers and the social work agencies of the country. This is also necessary if it has to perform the next and more difficult task of promoting co-ordination between social service agencies in the country.

Co-ordination as a concept has long been accepted as unexceptionable. It implies the utilization of available material and personnel resources in such a way that there is no duplication or overlapping and that the more urgent but less conspicuous problems are not left unnoticed in preference to less urgent but more easily perceived problems. No one will say that co-ordination should not be practised in any field, least of all in the field of social work. While the concept is readily accepted and repeatedly verbalized, its practice presents some real difficulty. The difficulty arises from the fact that social workers, like other human beings, get identified with their respective agencies sometimes almost to the exclusion of the objectives for which the agencies stand. From a purely rational point of view, we should all be ready to co-operate with whosoever is interested in doing the work that we ourselves would like to do. Purely rational considerations are not always decisive in guiding action, so that while we may agree that we should co-operate with other people we are also keen to retain our individuality as an organization because it is only thus that we can individually find recognition and fulfilment. Co-ordinated efforts require, in however small a degree, a readiness to share credit for achievement, and this is always accompanied by the fear that one may not receive any credit at all. Whenever a particular agency speaks of co-ordination, it is usually thinking in terms of other agencies co-operating and co-ordinating their efforts with its own. There seems to be so much in a name. The name and the auspices under which a particular activity is organized means much for the persons who are identified with that particular agency. No effort at co-ordination can therefore make any progress unless the reality of this situation has been taken into account. One important implication of this is that the agency which seeks to co-ordinate must be one with which other agencies are identified. They must feel that they have a "say" in the formation of its policy and that they generally stand to gain by working in collaboration with it. A national conference will be able to work as a co-ordinating organization only to the extent that it genuinely becomes representative of the points of view, the efforts, and the interests of its constituent organizations.

Co-ordination, moreover, involves not only a readiness on the part of individual agencies to pool their efforts together but also a development of a common awareness of the needs and the resources of the community. Fruitful co-ordination is possible only where the overall picture of social work needs and social resources is available and forms a part of the operating plan of the co-operating agencies. The programme of research and fact-finding that was emphasized earlier becomes therefore all the more significant in this context.

If a national conference succeeds in functioning as a forum of ideas, an educator of public opinion, an agency for fact-finding in social work, an instrument of technical guidance and a co-ordinating link for all social work effort, it will easily claim for itself the next important function of serving as a liaison between voluntary agencies and statutory welfare efforts. All over the world the sphere of interest of the state in the field of social welfare has continued to expand. Some states have set for themselves the objective of becoming a "welfare state". The undertaking of more and more activities by the state has meant the channelling of greater and greater resources through the agencies of the state. In this situation, there is a need for re-definition and re-statement of the role that voluntary agencies can play and should play in the growth of welfare services in the country. A national conference which can function as the spokesman of the voluntary sector can help in a clear statement of this role in a way that it will be acceptable to the state as well as to the voluntary agencies.

Even after delimiting the areas in which the state and the voluntary agencies can function independently, state action will stand in need of benefiting by close and continuous contact with the voluntary agencies and the community at large. A national conference can function as an interpreter of popular needs as well as of popular reactions to governmental measures.

These are a few of the objectives that the national conference of social work can set for itself. In the course of following through some of the latter objectives it may have been observed that some kind of an ongoing organization has been assumed. This needs a clearer statement. The term *conference* should normally refer only to a body which meets in periodic sessions. It does not usually connote an ongoing organization which undertakes "action" functions on a continual basis. In some countries there are councils of social service which usually look after the more active functions. But there is no hard and fast demarcation between the two types of organizations. What is important to realize is the need of fulfilling one minimum condition before the active, executive functions can be undertaken by a body which otherwise would devote itself primarily to deliberative functions. If a conference seeks to undertake the function of co-ordination—not only at the level of ideas, but in the field—it cannot do so unless it provides for a policy making and executive structure wherein every agency whose co-operation is desired is represented. And, this representation should not be merely for the purpose of participation in discussion but for the purpose of accepting commitments which will be honoured by the respective agencies. This is admittedly difficult. But this is necessary if the conference is to function as a co-coordinating and guidance-giving body.

Before closing this chapter I should make one thing clear. In describing the objectives I have stated what we should aim at. Obviously, no organization can achieve all those objectives from the day that it registers its articles of association. Conferring is a continuous and dynamic process and so is the education of public opinion—not to say anything of research and co-ordination. A national conference must therefore set itself to the pursuit of these objectives in the differing vicissitudes of successive decades and in the newer and different meanings that these objectives must undoubtedly achieve. May I express the hope that the National Conference of Social Work of Ceylon will succeed in setting the sights for social work endeavour in the country from year to year for many years, and will help in the process of continued achievement in this field.

CHAPTER TWELVE

PLANNING FOR SOCIAL WELFARE

Planning for social welfare is of recent origin. Not only because of its newness, but also because of the nature of social welfare activity, planning for social welfare presents some special problems. Planning in any field assumes that:

(i) there is a relatively clear definition of the objectives to be attained;
(ii) there is an assessment of the resources in men, materials, and money that can be utilized for the attainment of these objectives; and
(iii) the planning authority has the necessary sanctions and the skills which are required for the mobilization of resources in the attainment of the objectives specified.

These assumptions are never fully justified. Even in planning for economic development these conditions are met only partially. An effort will be made in this chapter to indicate why in the field of social welfare these conditions cannot be met even to the degree that they are in other fields.

One of the things that has historically characterized social welfare endeavour is its essential voluntariness. Social welfare effort has always been in the nature of a spontaneous response on the part of some individuals and groups to situations of need in their community. It is local in its inspiration as well as scope. Orphanages, widow homes and services providing outdoor relief to the destitute were established at different places in the country in response to immediate local needs. Questions regarding the total size of the problem, or of the number of services available to meet these needs were never raised. These questions were unimportant and irrelevant in respect of an effort which was essentially individual and which never aimed at seeking solutions to overall problems. It was an effort to render as much help and assistance as was possible within the available resources to such people as asked for it. It is only recently, with the initiation of state-financed services, that these questions have begun to be raised. For the first time, efforts are being made to organize services on a state-wide and even nation-wide scale. Even here the resources available are so limited that it often seems unimportant to some to find out the total size of any problem. The assumption probably is that the problems are admittedly too vast to be tackled with available resources and therefore an estimate of the exact size of the problem would only accentuate the sense of frustration in not having been able to achieve what is obviously necessary. The consequence is that, even at the end of two plan—periods, we are not hopeful of having the data which will enable us to obtain an overall perspective in the field of social welfare services. And yet, in the absence of such data, there can be no intelligent planning.

The nature of the origin of social welfare activity has also another consequence. Voluntary agencies and the individuals associated with them tend inevitably to focus on particular problems with which they have themselves been concerned. Very often individuals take to one activity rather than another due to wholly personal reasons. Thus, one may find persons who are interested only in the welfare of the blind, or the crippled, or the unmarried mothers. This tends to develop a limited outlook and often a false sense of priorities. The absence of objective data regarding the size of each problem, and its implications for national life, makes it possible for individuals to argue their own priorities to the exclusion of others. It is not unusual even at the highest level to find that individuals ride their own hobby horses and press their claims intolerantly for fear that they might otherwise suffer by default. It is therefore important that at least the bare minimum facts about our social problems be collected so that individuals charged with the responsibility for planning can develop an overall perspective and a legitimate sense of priorities between different fields of service.

It is, however, not enough to know what the problems are or how large they are. It is equally important to known the resources that are available for the solution of these problems. Most of the time a discussion on resources is devoted to the discussion of money resources available for the plan period. At least as important are the resources in men and organization. The implementation of the plans would depend upon the availability or personnel, whether paid or voluntary, trained or untrained. It is often assumed that once the services are created the personnel would become available. The experience has been that year after year services have had to be manned with persons who are not suitably equipped for the work that they are called upon to do. Except where the training programmes are directly financed out of state resources, there is often no liaison between the trainers and the planners. The trainers are unaware of the types of personnel that would be required and the numbers in which it would be called for. The planners are not aware of the different types to training programmes that exist and the rate of supply that these programmes can maintain over a period of time. This lack of co-ordination between planning and training must inevitably lead to ineffectiveness of the services organized and a consequent waste of funds.

The situation with regard to the assessment of organizational resources is even less satisfactory. One finds that funds are provided for schemes and programmes without a clear indication of the agencies that will undertake their implementation. The field where this has tended to happen most is that of youth welfare. The schemes for youth welfare are grouped separately for student youth and non-student youth. For student youth, it is assumed that the universities, colleges and schools will serve as the agencies for implementing the programmes. These latter are, however, never suitably equipped in terms of staff for undertaking extra-curricular activities of any magnitude. As a result, shortfalls in expenditure, indicative of non-implementation of programmes, are very common. In the case of non-student youth the difficulty is even greater. There are hardly one or two agencies which offer services in this area and even these agencies operate only one type of programme, viz., the organization of youth camps. This section of the youth therefore remains largely neglected despite financial provisions in the plan. An assessment of existing organizational resources and programmes to develop them further is therefore necessary if planning for social welfare is to be effective.

The third condition is that the planning authority should have the necessary sanctions and skills required for the mobilization and direction of existing resources. In so far as these resources consist of state funds, the condition can easily be met. In the field of social work, however, the resources also consist of volunteer individuals and organizations who are rendering services out of their own free will. In the last analysis, there can be no external sanctions that can be used for mobilizing them. In the sphere of economic activity the normal economic incentives for which individuals work provide a sufficient leverage to the state for influencing actions of private individuals and corporations. Since individuals cannot give up their economic pursuits except at a serious loss to themselves, the state can develop instruments of control which will direct this activity in one direction or another. This is not the case with private enterprise in the field of social welfare. The incentives that operate in this area are of a different order and therefore the instruments that will be utilized in directing voluntary activity in the field of social welfare will also have to be fashioned differently. The administrator in this area will have to possess an unusual degree of initiative, flexibility and leadership to be able to get a large number of independent, voluntary organizations to follow one overall pattern even when they pursue their own individual interests.

It is also important that if voluntary agencies are to fall in line with an overall plan of development they should be invited to participate in the process of planning itself. The efforts of the Working Group, set up at the Centre and also the corresponding Working Groups set up by state governments during the preparatory stages of the Third Plan, were intended to promote a sense of participation in the planning process on the part of the voluntary agencies. Since, however, the plan for welfare services as approved by the Planning Commission had little in common with the report of the Working Group, it can hardly be expected that the purpose of setting up the Working Groups was fulfilled.

The three points mentioned above refer primarily to the characteristics of voluntary endeavour in social welfare which if not taken into account might lead to difficulties in the way of effective planning in this field. There are some other factors which characterize our administrative and planning agencies and might have the same consequence if not taken into account. The first of these is lack of a sense of urgency in this filed. This follows from a somewhat misplaced sense of voluntariness that attaches to welfare services even when organized by the state. There is an assumption that welfare services are desirable but not necessary. They are often undertaken with a feeling that the government is really not called upon to do so. This attitude is unjustified and a remnant of the outmoded concepts of the limited responsibilities of the state. The lack of urgency is also a consequence of a lack of commitment on the part of the administrator. Typically, the welfare administrator, specially at the higher levels, is a person who has been transferred to this department as a matter of convenience. Neither his training nor his experience has usually equipped him specially for his new functions. He tends to look upon his office as one of the many that he is called upon to occupy in the course of a long administrative career. He does not have the kind of continuing interest which is likely to give him a sense of satisfaction in his work or to enable him to contribute by building on his experience from year to year.

Another characteristic of the governmental administrative agencies which is of interest here is their tendency, specially in recent years, to develop parallel programmes and services which are not necessarily co-ordinated with each other. In a large country such as ours, with its fast-growing bureaucratic organization, a certain degree of absence of co-ordination and duplication are probably unavoidable. But where the parallel developments are due not to unawareness of similar existing services but are a result of insistence on the part of each agency of its right to continue to offer similar programmes and services, we have a problem that must be taken note of. In at least four out of fourteen states we find that public funds are being simultaneously channelled through the State Welfare Advisory Boards and the Women's Welfare Departments for organizing welfare activities for women and children in the rural areas. The programmes of grants-in-aid are also being simultaneously administered by more than one governmental and statutory agency. If our scarce resources are to be utilized to the best advantage, it is imperative that better co-ordination is effected in the organization of welfare services. In the voluntary sector co-ordination is made difficult because of the identification of individuals with particular agencies and their zealousness to see that these agencies are individually recognized and established in the public mind. It seems that a similar phenomenon is at work even in the administrative agencies of the government.

The rapid expansion of welfare services under the auspices of the state is accompanied by some new problems. Unlike voluntary agencies which can arbitrarily decide which area or which problem they would tackle, the state agencies are required to cover as much of the country as possible and in as short a time as possible. The resources for such expansion of services are inevitably limited. This gives rise to the fictitious coverage of large areas by a few workers. So one hears of one project covering twenty-five villages or one worker covering ten villages. In practice it is impossible that the project or the worker could be effectively in touch with the communities and the households in their area. On the other hand, the claim to coverage gives a false sense of security and a feeling that we are nearer the achievement of our targets than we really are.

Another aspect of the same problem of limited resources is the paucity of trained personnel for manning a variety of different services offered by governmental agencies. Just as we seek to meet the problem of reaching as many communities as possible by fictitious coverage, we seek to meet the problem of a shortage of qualified personnel by conceiving of multipurpose workers. It is argued that a person who has had less than high school education and not more than nine months of job preparation can work as a health worker, educator, recreation worker and family counsellor. Obviously, again, our achievements in this direction must fall short of our expectations.

The need for training of persons is easily accepted, but we are unwilling to provide the resources in time and money to undertake proper training. Pressured by the need to meet plan targets we design training programmes varying from six weeks to six months. There is no clear understanding of who trains whom and for what purpose. It is assumed that the only things required in training are: a social work entrepreneur, a list of topics and a list of speakers.

There is a general recognition of the unsuitability of government departments for undertaking plan projects which require the exercise of initiative and quick action. In the economic field this recognition has been responsible for the establishment of corporations which enjoy a considerable measure of autonomy and freedom from day-to-day control. In the social welfare and cultural field this is parallelled by the emergence of the so-called voluntary bodies which are in effect government-nominated, registered bodies solely dependent upon government funds. This gives rise to a spurious kind of voluntariness and there will soon be a need now to distinguish between "public" registered and "private" registered societies.

The above are a few of the factors that make for difficulties and blemishes that characterize our planning for social welfare. These cannot be attributed entirely to lack of experience. The exercise of repeated planning for successive five-year periods will not by itself help us to overcome them. They have consciously to be taken note of and counteracted in the interests of the individuals and groups that stand in need of the services.

CHAPTER THIRTEEN

ORGANIZATIONAL AND ADMINISTRATIVE FRAMEWORK OF PLANNING SOCIAL SERVICES

The Planning Commission

The organizational and administrative framework for social planning in India is provided by the Planning Commission which was brought into existence in March 1950. The Planning Commission is concerned primarily with the preparation of plans for the economic development of the country, but economic development cannot be wholly separated from the development of human resources with which social services are directly concerned. The three successive Five-Year Plans formulated by the Planning Commission have shown an awareness of the vital importance of the human factor in development and of the need to provide services in this sector. The functions of the Planning Commission provide that it will undertake to:

1. Assess the existing resources.
2. Formulate a plan for their most efficient utilization.
3. Define stages by which the plan should be carried out.

---

*A note prepared for incorporation in the National Report on India compiled by the Indian Conference of Social Work and submitted to the Athens session of the International Conference of Social Work, 1964.

4. Indicate the factors that may retard or promote economic development.
5. Determine the type of machinery needed for the execution of the plan.
6. Appraise, periodically, the progress of the plan.
7. Recommend such interim or additional measures as might be necessary from time to time.

The work of the Planning Commission is organized in three separate branches: (i) the General Secretariat which looks after all the administrative work; (ii) the Technical Divisions which do the actual work of scrutinizing various proposals in each sector of developmental activity and prepare drafts for the consideration of the Commission (the Technical Divisions also conduct studies relating to Plan Projects and prepare study materials); and (iii) the Programme Administration Division where senior officers who function as advisers help the Commission by keeping it informed of the progress and implementation of the various schemes, and of the problems of finance associated with the plan as a whole.

The Planning Commission has the Prime Minister of India as its chairman. It has a full-time Deputy Chairman and may have six or seven members in charge of technical subjects or some aspects of planning such as administration, finance, etc. The subjects of health, education, social welfare, welfare of the backward classes, rehabilitation and housing, which are mainly covered under the term "social services", are divided between different members depending upon the composition of the Commission at a particular time and the interests of the individual members of the Commission. Even in the organization of technical work the social service subjects are divided into six different divisions, viz., Education, Health and Local Self-Government, Labour and Employment, Prohibition, Public Co-operation, and Social Welfare. Each of these divisions is headed by either a Chief, a Director or an Assistant Chief depending upon the scope of its work. These officers are supported by technical staff designated as Senior Research Officers, Research Officers and Technical Assistants.

Formulation of Plan Proposals

In a sense, specific plan proposals may be said to originate in these Technical Divisions. But the divisions do not work by themselves. The ministries of the Central Government which are concerned with these subjects are directly involved in the process of planning. The usual procedure is to set up Working Groups consisting of representatives of the concerned ministries, the Technical Divisions of the Planning Commission, and non-official members who are selected on the basis of their familiarity with the particular subject with which a Working Group is concerned. These Working Groups, which are constituted about two years prior to the finalization of the plan by the Commission, prepare draft proposals for its consideration. They also review the operation of the various schemes in the preceding plan, obtain views from state governments and other concerned agencies and prepare a report setting forth a series of developmental proposals which are formulated on the assumption that a certain quantum of resources is going to be available for the implementation of the proposals outlined. Since the Working Groups include persons who have a special interest in their particular area—whether it be housing, social welfare or education—they tend to be unduly optimistic about the size of the resources likely to be available to them. At any rate, they consider it important that they should always ask for a resource allocation much greater than they need or can effectively utilize.

When all the proposals made by the different Working Groups are put together, they are usually found to be far in excess of the total resources available for the entire plan. The process of pruning is an inevitable part of the process of planning. This work is done at various levels—by divisional heads, by the Senior Administrative Officers of the Commission, and finally by the Commission itself. One of the unfortunate and unanticipated consequences of this process of pruning is that when it is undertaken by people who have not been associated in the initial formulation of the various schemes, it is likely to upset the original priorities and, in some instances, introduce an imbalance in all the proposals put forth by individual Working Groups.

The Problems of Co-ordination

One of the problems of planning at the national level is the difficulty in ensuring co-ordination and reaching an agreement on priorities between different agencies, and the different levels of the same agency, which are responsible for implementing the programme. In the field of social services, this difficulty is accentuated by two factors: (i) that most of the subjects covered under the term "social services" are subjects which are the responsibility of state governments and, in some cases, of local self-government bodies; and (ii) that the agencies responsible for the implementation of the plan schemes are not necessarily governmental agencies, and are therefore not subject to manipulation or direction by the planning authorities.

We will consider first the problem of co-ordinating central and state government efforts in planning. In order to help the central and state governments to arrive at a general agreement in overall policies and national priorities, the members of the Planning Commission use the forum of the National Development Council. This Council, which has the Prime Minister as its chairman, has a membership made up of the Chief Ministers of all state governments, senior members of the Central Cabinet and all the members of the Planning Commission. All major issues of national policy relating to economic and social development are discussed in the Council and the decisions arrived at become morally binding upon the planners as well as the participating governments, though the Council itself has no statutory basis.

When an agreement on overall priorities has been reached, there is still need for consensus on programmes. Here, the difficulty is partially overcome by letting the states have their own plans of development and by setting aside a portion of the total resources for state plans. These state schemes are distinguished form the centrally sponsored schemes though, in both instances, the actual implementation has to be done in the states. The pattern of financing the state and the central schemes is usually different though in some cases even the state schemes may be largely financed out of the resources made available by the Centre. The division of developmental plans into those sponsored by the states and those sponsored by the Centre allows for some difference of opinion between the Commission and the state governments with regard to the validity as well as the primacy of particular programmes.

In spite of these measures, however, there is still scope for a feeling that planning at the national level involves a certain measure of centralization and that the Planning Commission, and indirectly the Central Government, tend to influence and restrict the freedom of state governments through the control of financial resources. The lack of agreement between the Planning Commission and the state governments is sometimes a factor responsible for lukewarmness with which individual schemes may be treated at the state level.

The problem of co-ordinating the activities of governmental and non-governmental agencies is in some ways more difficult than the problem of co-ordinating the activities of the central and the state governments. In the field of social services voluntary agencies play an important part. Particularly within the field of social welfare, as different from the areas of health and education, the needs as well as the difficulty of co-ordinating governmental action with voluntary effort are all the greater. The Planning Commission attempts to establish a liaison between governmental efforts and those of voluntary agencies in three ways:

1. By associating non-governmental agencies and non-officials in the process of planning.
2. By entrusting some government-sponsored programmes to voluntary agencies for implementation.
3. By promoting the growth of voluntary agencies through a programme of grants-in-aid.

At the level of planning the Commission invites representatives of voluntary agencies and individual non-officials to work on some of their committees. Apart from the Working Group on Social Welfare, which is set up jointly by the Ministry of Education and the Planning Commission, there is a special Advisory Committee on Public Co-operation which functions within the Planning Commission itself. On both these bodies, non-officials are represented.

Such association of representatives of voluntary agencies does not really go very far in bringing the total voluntary effort in the country into line with the overall programmes visualized by the government. This is a natural consequence of the fact that voluntary agencies are themselves not sufficiently organized as a body and have not succeeded in developing broad national policies. As a result, the individuals who sit on the various advisory committees are not really in a position to speak on behalf of the voluntary sector as a whole, nor even to indicate what the overall thinking of voluntary agencies is on matters of policy.

The government can also influence and co-ordinate the actions of voluntary agencies through the manipulation of its grants-in-aid programme. To the extent that voluntary agencies need governmental assistance, their efforts can be channelized into areas for which such governmental assistance is available. To some extent the overall policies of the Central Social Welfare Board, which is the main grant-giving agency of the government in the welfare field, do tend to influence voluntary agencies in this manner. But here, two difficulties arise: first, there is absence of a clear governmental policy in the area of social welfare which leads grant-giving bodies to take ad hoc decisions which do not always fall into a pattern; and, secondly, since the grant-giving bodies themselves function as parts of different ministries, their actions cannot always be co-ordinated with each other even if there is such a policy.

Plan Follow-up and Evaluation

The Planning Commission keeps in touch with the implementation of the plan in many ways. The Programme Administration of the Planning Commission is directly concerned with the progress registered in the attainment of plan targets in different sectors. This branch of the Planning Commission remains in continuous contact with the various ministries of the Central Government which in their turn are in communication with the concerned departments at the state level. The Technical Divisions also keep themselves informed of the progress made and the problems faced in the implementation of the plan. Besides, though the plan is formulated on a five-year basis, financial sanctions are issued for one year at a time. The individual departments and ministries of the central and state governments and representatives of the Planning Commission get together every year for annual plan discussions. At this point, the Planning Commission gets the opportunity to influence effectively the actions of the executive agencies of the government. The major consideration naturally is whether the financial allocations made in the previous year have been fully utilized for the purposes for which they were earmarked. Demands for the ensuing year are sought to be related to the performance of the previous one. This, however, is not easy to do because the states which are most in need of particular services are the ones that have the greatest difficulty in providing the necessary organizational resources to provide them. These discussions also provide an opportunity to the state governments to urge a reconsideration of original priorities and a re-allocation of some sub-heads and schemes within a major subject area.

In addition to the annual plan discussions, there are also special conferences and meetings that are organized by the Planning Commission to enable different state governments to compare notes and to enable the Commission itself to have an overall view of the developments taking place in different parts of the country. During the third year of the plan, the Planning Commission organizes a mid-term appraisal of the achievements and shortfalls. This is a point at which major decisions may be made about a change of emphasis in projects and about re-allocation of funds from one head to another. The members of the Planning Commission as well as the members of the

National Development Council participate in such mid-term appraisals.

The Planning Commission also benefits by the work of the Committee on Plan Projects and the Programme Evaluation Organization. The Committee on Plan Projects has been appointed by the National Development Council. It is a high-powered body consisting of persons chosen from amongst members of the Central Cabinet, Chief Ministers of states, and Members of Parliament. This committee appoints study teams to undertake a review of the progress registered in particular sectors of the plan and to recommend ways of ensuring economy and efficiency. The reports of this committee are considered both by the National Development Council and the Planning Commission and in some cases they have led to major changes of policy.

The Programme Evaluation Organization is primarily a research organization which undertakes annual as well as ad hoc surveys of the Community Development Programmes in the rural areas. It has published annual reports since 1953 and has additionally made available reports on particular aspects of developmental work in the villages.

Neither the Committee on Plan Projects nor the Programme Evaluation Organization is subordinate to the Planning Commission. The latter, however, is more directly associated with the Planning Commission, being a body made up of full-time officers. The Planning Commission takes note of the observations of both these organizations in the formulation of its plans and in the periodic review to which they are subjected.

INDEX

Index